THE 333 BOOK

333 LICKS, TRICKS & TECHNIQUES EVERY GUITARIST SHOULD KNOW

Mike Ihde

Distributed by,

Mel Bay Publications, Inc.

#4 Industrial Drive

Pacific, MO 63069-0066

USA

1-800-8-MEL-BAY (1-800-863-5229)

Find them on the web at http://www.melbay.com/

Published by My Guy Music

ISBN 978-0-615-20858-9

Printed and bound in the United States of America by Kingprinting.com

I

DEDICATION

This book is dedicated to Maureen. Without her endless love, guidance, support and confidence in my ability to complete this project, you wouldn't be reading this.

Very special thanks to Mark French for all his technical support, Barrie Nettles for his friendship and common sense, Bill Leavitt for inspiring and guiding me to write my first two books and whose presence is felt on every page, Barrie Nettles and Steve Pina for their invaluable proofreading skills, Annmarie Morawiak for the photography, Peter Troisi for his ears, Bob Cooper for playing piano on some of the examples, Michelle Morawiak for the musical quotes, Steve Pina for letting me borrow some of his guitars, Pete Huttlinger, David Scher and Larry Baione for their help.

My undying love goes out to the members of my first band, "The Uncalled Four" (Eddie "Elliot" Karlan on drums, Joe Reilly on rhythm guitar and Charlie Bogden on bass) who started me on this magical, musical journey.

My most sincere thanks to all the artists who donated their time and talent to the video performance/interviews. I wanted you to see and hear as many different players in as many different styles on as many different instruments as possible. Hopefully, after viewing their video segments, you'll want to know more about them, their music and their instruments. You may even be tempted to try some of it yourself.

ABOUT THE RECORDINGS:

I want you to hear how each example sounds in the context of a real band, not just by itself, so each example has a full band track backing me up. Most examples have a few bars of me playing improvised solos before and after the written lick.

If you have trouble playing them at the recorded tempo, use a software program to slow them down.

TECHNICAL STUFF:

All the examples were recorded in Digital Performer on my Mac. Sibelius was used for the music and tab notation. Photoshop was used to create each page. Guitar Rig by Native Instruments was used on many of the guitar tracks. Band in a Box by PG Music was used for some of the drum and piano backgrounds. The drum sounds are from FXpansion's BFD drum module. Other sounds are from the Miroslav Philharmonik, Native Instruments Bandstand and Akousitik Piano modules as well as a Korg N5ex keyboard.

Guitars used include an Epiphone Emperor, Fender Telecaster (one with and one without a B-Bender), Fender Jaguar, Fender Stratocaster, Godin xtSA, Martin Acoustic, Variax Acoustic 700 and a Roland G-303 guitar (without the synth).

• IMPORTANT •

The DVD in this book will NOT play in your consumer DVD player. It is formatted for your computer, either PC or Mac.

Open the "Audio Folder" and put the 240 MP3's into a new folder you create named "333 audio." Import that folder into iTunes, your iPod or any program used to play MP3 audio.

In the "Video Folder" there are 15 QuickTime movies. You can click on any one to watch it. If you want to watch them from your consumer DVD player, drag the files to your desktop and burn them onto a recordable blank DVD.

PREFACE

I wrote this book to open your eyes and ears to as many styles of guitar music as possible in one publication. I admit that I tend to oversimplify everything, but when you strip a particular style down to the bare bones to see what makes it tick, you'll find it's not all that complicated. Sure, creating music that comes from your heart, finding your own voice as a guitarist and being able to move people with your music is a life long journey, but if you don't learn all the stylistic licks that define a given style it will take you a lot longer to reach your goal. If you really work hard on the material in this book, you *will* be ready for any gig or recording session you come across.

The "Licks" in this book will teach you how to phrase in a wide variety of useful styles. I strongly suggest that you do more research of a given style on your own. Listen to the great players, buy other books that are dedicated solely to one style and most importantly, learn what makes a style work. Rip it apart and see what's inside. Don't just learn a lick because it sounds good, learn *why* it sounds good. Then, and only then, will you have actually learned something about the style that you can use.

The "Tricks" part of the book will show you a lot of fun and useful (and some useless) sounds you can make on the guitar without having to spend a nickel on outboard equipment.

The "Techniques" part of the book will give you a solid foundation in theory for chord scales, rhythm guitar styles, scale fingerings, chord forms and more.

Rather than put each style or topic into a chapter or group them together, I chose to mix everything up and scatter them around the book so that each page would have something new and different on it.

You should start at number 1 and not stop until you get to number 333. Find a teacher to help you if you need it. Try to copy the sound, phrasing and emotion of the material on the recordings.

Thanks for buying my book, have fun with it and check out my web site www.mikeihde.com for info on my other books and CDs. If you have questions about anything in this book, please send me an e-mail at The333Book@comcast.net. I'll be happy to answer all the questions you may have.

ABOUT THE AUTHOR

I was born and raised in Nutley, New Jersey, once voted the safest town in the USA and home to such notables as sharpshooter Annie Oakley, actor Robert Blake and domestic guru Martha Stewart.

I started playing guitar when I was 13 and joined my first band, "The Uncalled Four" at 16. After graduation from High School, I went to the Art Students League in New York City in hopes of becoming a commercial artist, all the while playing at High School dances and a club or two when they didn't check our ID.

After becoming disillusioned about the struggle of the life of a commercial artist, I wasn't sure what to do next. Luckily, my Mother had heard about a school in Boston called Berklee School of Music (it hadn't earned the name "College" yet). I graduated in 1972 and have been teaching there ever since! Yes, that's a long time, but I actually do love my job. It's a good gig!

Over the years I've played with a lot of fantastic musicians and had the privilege of teaching many students who have gone on the do great things on their instrument, as vocalists or in the music business as songwriters, arrangers and producers.

My love for all styles of music has made me a versatile guitar player and vocalist and keeps me giging in a wide variety of performance situations. I have two other books, "Country Guitar Styles" and "Rock Guitar Styles" available through my web site, www.mikeihde.com as well as a CD and music/tab for the lap steel called "A Different Slant." By the way, my last name is pronounced "eyed."

Career-wise, I've played pedal steel with Joan Baez and the Boston Pops at Symphony Hall in Boston with John Williams conducting, wrote, performed and recorded the score for the documentary, "The Sun Dagger" with Robert Redford narrating which aired nationally on PBS, taught guitar in Japan, had two Gospel songs recorded in Nashville, played on the theme for the TV show "Home Again" with Bob Vila, gave guitar and pedal steel lessons to Joe Perry of Aerosmith and so much more than I have room to list here.

Keep your ears and your mind open to all styles and never say, "I hate that kind of music" because someday, someone may want to pay you a lot of money to play that style, and it would be a drag if you didn't know how.

NOTATION LEGEND

My system for notating bends is a little different than the way others do it but I believe it's a natural extension of our standard notation system.

 **The Slur:** By definition, don't attack the next note. On guitar the only way to do this is to hammer-on. Going in the other direction would mean to pull-off.

 **The Gliss (glissando):** Slide your finger from one note to the other and pick both notes.

 **Slur and Gliss:** Slide between the notes and don't pick the second note.

 **The Grace Note:** A hammer-on or pull-off played very quickly just before the target note sounds.

 **The Bend:** Play the first note and bend it to the second. In the Tab, the target note is written smaller because it indicates the fret of the bent pitch, not the fret of the finger.

 **The Pre-Bend:** Bend before you pick the note and then release downwards. In the Tab, the larger number shows the fret your finger is on, the smaller note is the fret the pitch is on.

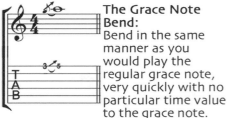 **The Grace Note Bend:** Bend in the same manner as you would play the regular grace note, very quickly with no particular time value to the grace note.

 **The Unison Bend:** Bend F to G on the third string while holding G on the second string until they become the same pitch.

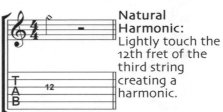 **Natural Harmonic:** Lightly touch the 12th fret of the third string creating a harmonic.

 **Artificial or Fingered Harmonic:** Fret the note normally then lightly touch 12 frets above that note with your first finger while picking with either your thumb or pick.

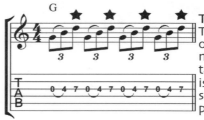 **Tapping:** The tap is indicated by a (★) star over the note to be tapped. The normal pattern is pick, hammer-on, tap then repeat. The middle finger is suggested as the tapping finger so you don't have to change the position of your pick.

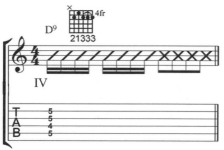

Rhythm Chord Slashes: The slashes show you the rhythm to be played and which chords should sound and which should be dead, the chord form box shows the chord fingering, the position mark tells you which fret your first finger is on and the Tab shows you which frets the pitches are found on.

Roman Numerals:

I = I	XI = 11
II = 2	XII = 12
III = 3	XIII = 13
IV = 4	XIV = 14
V = 5	XV = 15
VI = 6	XVI = 16
VII = 7	XVII = 17
VIII = 8	XVIII = 18
IX = 9	XIX = 19
X = 10	XX = 20

Roman Numerals are used to indicate what position to play in.

Position is defined as what fret your first finger is on. In 5th position (V) your first finger is on the 5th fret, 2nd finger on the 6th, 3rd finger on the 7th and 4th finger on the 8th.

Any other notational issues are explained in the descriptions preceding a particular example.

 The example is recorded and can be found in the audio folder with the same number as the example.

 The example is recorded and can be found in the audio folder plus it's explained further in the video folder. Open "Mike Ihde."

 The example is only found in the video folder. Open "Mike Ihde"

1

Licks using open strings have a very special sound. If you play just the pitches without the open strings, you'll notice it's nothing more than a descending G major scale. *But*, when you add in the open strings and carefully follow the fingering, you have a completely different sounding lick. The most important part is to let all the fingered notes continue to ring out until the last possible second before you have to let them go in order to get to the next note. For example, the F♯ on the "and" of beat 2 in the first measure should ring until the note B comes in on the "and" of beat 4. Also, the first note B rings out for one and half beats. This kind of lick works well in Country, Pop or Jazz ballads.

All open strings must ring throughout the example.

2

One day when a student missed his lesson, I was looking in my desk drawer to see if I had anything interesting to stick in the strings. I found a piece of electrical wire that had been attached to a lamp. There were 2 rubber coated wires joined together. I pulled them apart so I'd only have one piece, cut it to about 4 inches in length and wove it, over/under, into the strings. I was amazed to hear that my guitar sounded *a lot* like a banjo! Play ex. 292 with this attachment and listen for yourself. Here's what it looks like...

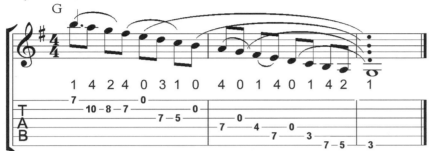

3

The whole tone scale. The dom⁷♯5 chord, also called dom⁷(aug), dom⁷(aug5), dom⁷(+5) or dom⁷(♭13), usually takes a whole tone scale. It's a 6 note scale made up of whole steps (2 frets). Just for the sake of trying something new, throw it in over a dom⁷ chord at the end of a phrase and you'll make people sit up and listen. F.S. means "finger stretch." Keep your hand in position and stretch to get the note.

CHICKEN PICKIN':

I don't know if this is how it happened, but it could have....A guy is sitting on his front porch playing his guitar, there are clucking chickens all over the place, he tries to imitate them on the guitar by making a sound that mimics their clucking. He plays: puck-puck-a-puck-aat, and Chicken Pickin' was invented! However it happened, it's one of the most used sounds in Country Music. There are several ways of creating the right sound, for this one, use the pinch harmonic technique (see ex. 166 for more). Choke up on the pick so that very little of it is visible. This is the original Chicken Pickin' lick. Bend the last note up slowly for about a half step or so.

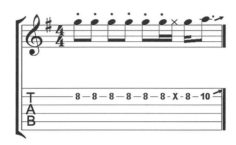

The second most common Chicken Pickin' lick is this one. Prebend a note then release it slowly. The idea here is that on the downstroke you sit on the string you just picked with the side of your thumb so no pitch is heard, just a dead click. The upstroke, however, is picked normally so you can hear the pitch. The hard part is to release the bend slowly and evenly while chopping away with your picking hand. Practice a scale and play each note twice, once with a dead downstroke and once with a normal upstroke. The second part of the example uses dead triplets. These are harder to control but sound really good.

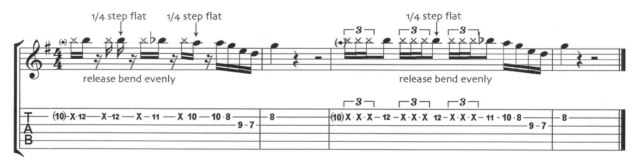

Another way to Chicken Pick is to finger the notes but not fret them. This gives the illusion of the actual pitches. Try picking with the Rock style pinch harmonic technique (see ex. 166 for more). It will make the notes pop out a little better.

Examples 4, 5 and 6 are played back to back on the recording.

7

A nice Lydian lick for the end of a Jazz tune. The band is holding the final Fmaj⁷ chord and you throw in this lick. Very cool. The addition of the chromatic notes at the end is a nice touch.

It was written by William G. Leavitt, the Chairman of the Guitar Department at Berklee College of Music from 1965 to 1990. His books, "A Modern Method For Guitar", Vol. 1, 2 and 3 are available from Berklee Press and have become the bible for guitar instruction around the world.

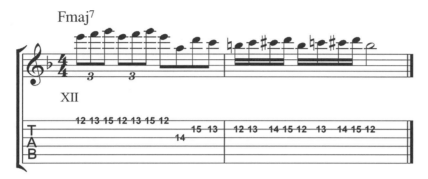

8

A good blues lick for the end of the 12 bar pattern. Reminiscent of sax or piano lines, you're chromatically approaching the third of each chord at the start of the lick and then chromatically approaching the flat seventh at the end of each phrase.

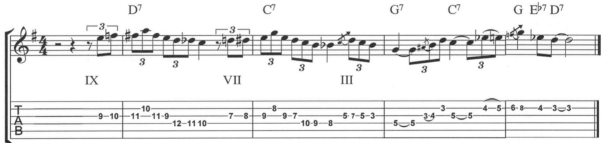

9

This Fusion lick uses a 4 part chord arpeggio over a dominant 7th chord technique. You'll notice as you go through the book that all the cool sounding Jazz and Fusion licks seem to happen over some form of a dominant 7th chord. That's because you can get away with so much more on that kind of chord. If you have a major 7th chord to play over, your only choices are the Ionian or Lydian mode. If you were to start playing all these weird constant structure parallel things over a major 7th chord you'll get stuff thrown at you...by other band members!

12 BAR BLUES PROGRESSIONS:

Most Blues tunes are written in a 12 bar form. You *must* memorize these progressions and be able to play them in any key. The following examples get progressively more complicated. You can play the C Blues scale (see ex. 49) over all of these progressions, but trying to catch some of the chord tones of the "other" chords will make you sound like you actually know what you're doing.

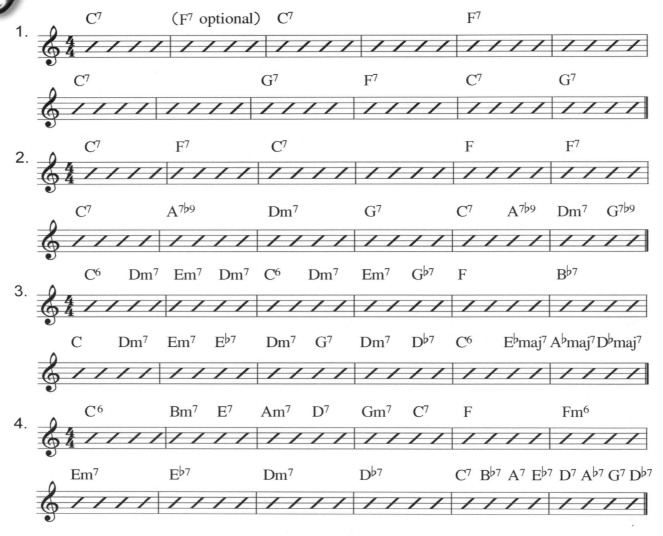

ADJACENT STRING LEGATO PHRASING EXERCISE: When 2 notes occur next to each other on adjacent strings, you don't lift your finger or keep it barred, you roll it from one note to the next. It's the only way to make a smooth transition with no silence between the notes. This exercise will help a lot. When you roll up to a higher string you simultaneously lay down your finger and roll it onto the next note. Keep the back edge of your finger barely touching the string you're leaving to mute it. When going to a lower string, you start with your finger a little flat on the high note so you have some room to stand it up on the lower note. Remember, don't let any 2 notes ring together and make sure there's no silence between any 2 notes.

Dominant 7 with 13 is a good substitute for a plain old dom^7 chord. You can use 13 if the dom^7 chord is a I^7, II^7, IV^7, V^7 or any dom^7 who's root is nondiatonic like E$^{\flat 7}$ or D$^{\flat 7}$ in the key of C. The sus^4 (or suspended 4) chord replaces the 3rd degree of the chord with the 4th degree. This gives an unstable sound (sub-dominant) that usually resolves back to the original dom^7 chord. The dom^{9}sus^4 has become the V chord of choice for practically every Pop ballad. It is often written as F/G instead of calling it a G^{9}sus^4. It has the quality of the IIm^7 chord and should be treated like one for the chord scale. In other words, a G^{9}sus^4 chord will take a D Dorian mode.

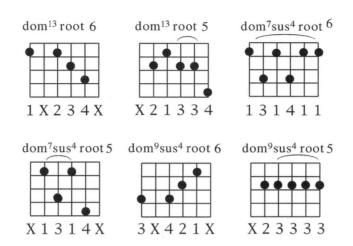

This is a quick little Country ending lick with a sweep arpeggio at the end. Play it fast and clean. ⊓=downstroke, ∨ = upstroke.

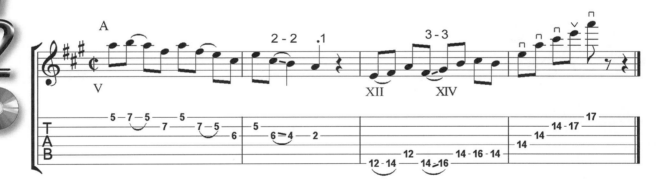

HELPFUL HINT:
When you have to read a complicated sixteenth note melody like the one below, just multiply everything by 2. One measure of hard to read rhythms will become 2 measures of much easier to read rhythms. After a while, you'll get used to these sixteenth rhythms and be able to "see" them as easy eighth note rhythms. Just do 15 minutes of reading practice every day and you'll be amazed at how fast you get better at it.

Any volume is too loud for somebody.

13

The harmonic minor scale can be thought of as a major scale with a flat 3rd and a flat 6th, or a natural minor scale with a raised 7th degree. Harmonic minor is often used on a dom$^{7\flat 9}$ chord. The modal name for this would be Mixolydian $\flat$2, $\flat$6. In this example, it's a G Mixolydian $\flat$2, $\flat$6 mode or a C harmonic minor scale. The rule is: If the chord is a $\flat$9/$\flat$13 chord or a III^7, VI^7 or VII^7, play harmonic minor from the intended tonic or up a perfect fourth. Don't forget, F.S. means "finger stretch," stretch your first finger to get to the note without moving the rest of your hand.

14

Here is one of the all time classic pedal steel licks. It's a little unusual because you're bending the "other way." It may take a little time to get used to this but it's worth it. As with all Country licks, make sure it's perfectly in tune. When your 3rd finger plays the G and your 4th finger plays the C, let them ring throughout the measure.

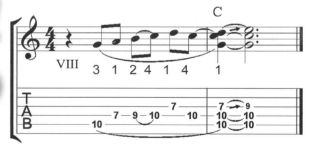

15

A nice minor Jazz lick. Adding the major 7th note against the minor 7th chord gives it a special sound. You could say you're using a B major triad arpeggio over the Em^7 chord.

16 The "add 2" chord has become the Pop ballad chord of choice. Whenever you have to play any kind of Pop or Country ballad and all you see on the chord chart is a G major chord, substitute the "add 2" chord and the producer will think you're a genius. I call these *real guitar chords* because they are voicings specific to the instrument. They contain open strings which means in order to play the same chords in other keys, you must use a capo (see ex.223). As a matter of fact, most of these chords sound better with the capo on the 5th fret or higher. You can strum them or arpeggiate them like a piano player would.

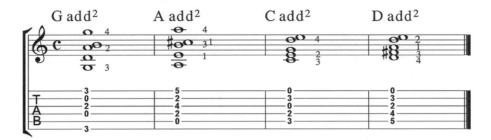

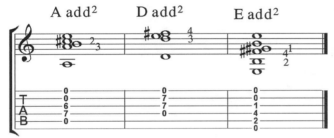

These chords are called "add 2" rather than "add 9" to indicate that the 2nd degree is placed next to the 3rd degree in the voicing. This creates the nice buzz of that whole step between the 2nd and 3rd degrees.
If you called it "add 9" the 9th could be voiced in any octave.

17 This Jazz example has some complicated lines over an A⁷ chord. Lots of nice shapes to dissect and use elsewhere. As you learn more examples like this one, you'll begin to see the common thread that runs through them. Always try to use lots of chromatics and approach notes (see ex. 81, 82, 83 and 84 for more) interspersed with arpeggios.

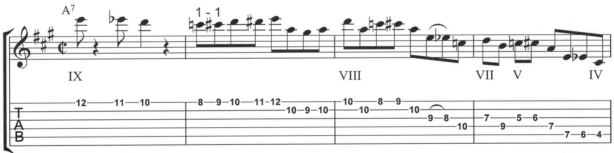

DRUM STICK RHYTHM GUITAR:

That's right, playing rhythm guitar with a drum stick is a pretty cool sound. Talk about attack! You just can't get this kind of sound from a pick. Hold the drumstick like you would a pencil (see photo) and bang it on the strings, hitting them all at the same time. It will take some practice to get the precise rhythms shown here, but with a little bit of work, you should be drumming your way to new rhythms in no time at all.

The first example is the classic Spanish sounding flamenco style chords you might hear in a tune like *Malagueña*. The second example is more of a funk groove.

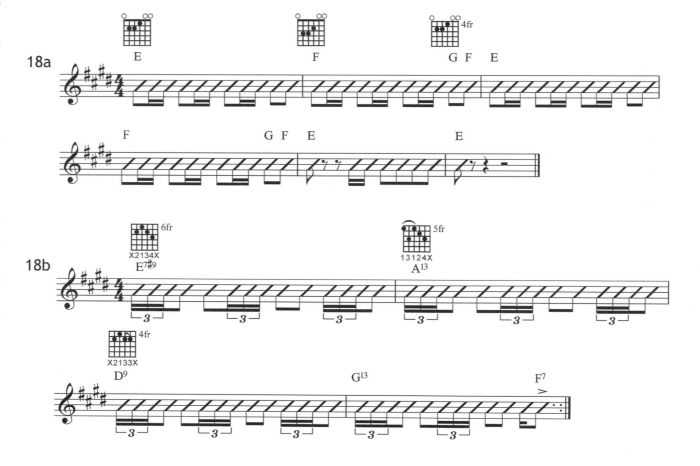

COOL "GUITAR CHORDS" USING OPEN STRINGS:

Examples 1 and 2 are big and pretty sounding major 7th and minor 9th voicings. Turn on the chorus and use a stereo amp setup and it's huge! Anytime you can add an open string to a chord it always sounds good. If that produces half or whole steps between the voices that's even better and actually, that's the point of trying to do it this way. Example 3 are triads over a bass note (no third) which creates a new chord rich in tensions. Example 4 is some other chords you should know and a few inversions of an E chord. The last chord is my favorite "what the heck is that" chord. I learned it from the old TV show *Peter Gunn*. As they went to commercial, the guitarist would strum this chord. Since I was maybe 13 when this show was on, it took me weeks to get all the notes (no TiVo back then). This is just a small sample of the hundreds of really nice chords you can create by using open strings in your voicings or by placing a chord over a bass note and then analyzing what the new voicing becomes.

2 0 0

This Jazz lick uses a whole tone scale on the G7#5 chord but breaks it up into 4 note groups. It then moves that group up the neck in whole steps and adds the final A# to make for a smooth resolution to the 7th of the Cmaj7 chord.

2 1 1

Here's an open string Country lick on a D7 chord. These are used quite often by all the hot Nashville pickers. Keep the fingered notes down until you have to move them. Let the open strings ring throughout the example. These open string licks have a pattern that shows up all the time. They come in 3 note groups. Usually, it's 2 notes followed by an open string. Just remember to let notes ring into the following note. Let the first note A ring into the F#, let the F# ring into the open E etc.

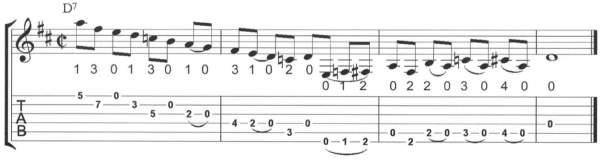

2 2 2

As we all know, it's more important to look good (on stage) than to sound good. So here is a lick that has absolutely no intrinsic value except that it looks impressive on stage. You can see that melodically there's nothing going on. The lick is played by using a different finger on each note. Warning...don't use this lick in the recording studio!

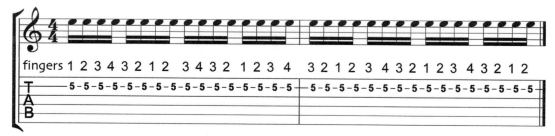

23

This is one of those, if-you-can-play-it-fast-enough-it-will-sound-cool kind of licks. It will sound good in almost any style but seems more at home in Jazz. The chords don't matter much because you're playing so chromatically. Just make sure you resolve it to a good note on the last chord.

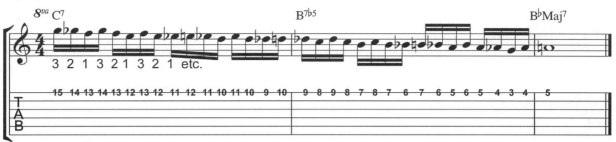

24

A Jazz riff over an B⁷ chord. Opening with a scale in thirds and then a C#m⁷ arpeggio followed by a B⁷ arpeggio. As with a lot of these Jazz licks, even though the band may be swinging, you're playing straight eighths, it's just what those Jazz guys do.

25

The dom⁷ augmented chord can be written as dom⁷⁽♯⁵⁾, dom⁷+, dom⁷(aug.), or dom⁷⁽⁺⁵⁾. Whichever way it's written, it is still built from the root, 3rd, sharped 5th, and flat 7th of a major scale. It's usually used on a V⁷ chord to add a stronger melodic resolution to the I chord. It also shows up as an available tension on a III⁷, VI⁷ and VII⁷ chord. Enharmonically, it can be called dom⁷⁽♭¹³⁾ and that would take a melodic minor scale a perfect 4th above the chord name. The dom⁷aug chord takes a whole tone scale (see ex. 3 and ex. 56). Dom⁷♭5 is often interchangeable with a dom⁷♯5 chord.

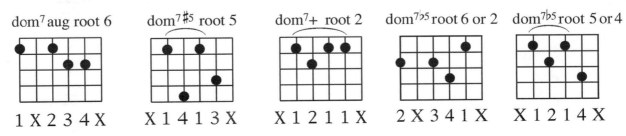

You're never more than one fret away from a right note.

Walking bass and chords in a Blues progression. There are many ways of playing a cool walking bass line at the same time as the rhythm chords in a blues progression, but most of them are fairly difficult to play. This one is *easy*. There are only 4 basic shapes you need to know in order to play this entire example. Shape one is the first F^7 chord. Shape two is on beat 2 of the first measure (an E$^\flat$ triad in first inversion). That shape is moved up chromatically until it's the next inversion of the F chord you started with. The whole process is repeated in measure 2 on the IV chord. Shape three is on beat 3 of the 4th measure (an F^7 chord). Shape 4 is the E$^{\flat 7}$ chord on beat 2 of measure 8. That's all there is. Make sure your pinky never leaves the 3rd string. On the recording, I played it as written the first time followed by the rhythm shown at the end of the example.

4th finger stays on 3rd string throughout

Play the example 3 ways: first, as written with a pick, second, as written with just fingers and third, with fingers using the rhythm below. Your fretting hand plays just like the written version but your picking hand breaks it up to sound like two parts, rhythm and bass.

Reading or playing in odd time signatures usually strikes fear into the hearts of most musicians. As a rule, odd time signatures can be broken down into smaller groups that are much easier to play. This classic 5/4 rhythm is the same as a measure of 3/4 followed by a measure of 2/4. It's almost always split up this way and is usually played with a swing feel.

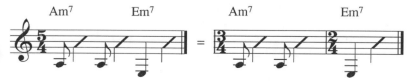

288

This Jazz lick uses a diminished 7th arpeggio running up the neck through all its inversions and finally resolving to the root of the C⁶ chord.

It's also a good cross picking exercise. The leaps between the first and fourth string can be a problem. Start slow and gradually work the tempo up until you're really flying. As always, a metronome is critical. Find a metronome marking that you can comfortably play this example at, than every few days, move it up a few numbers. You'll be amazed that within a few weeks you may have doubled the tempo you started with.

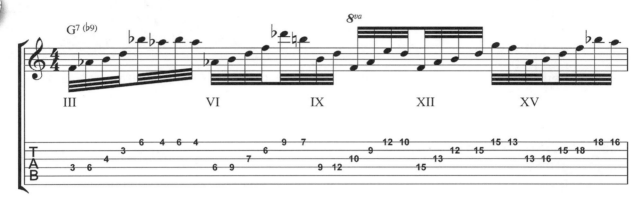

289

Here's one of those "out" sounding Fusion licks. I always thought, when I heard things like this, that the player had simply moved everything up a fret just to make it sound strange and then brought it back down to resolve it. I still think that's what they do. How else can you explain that the section starting on the A♭ note uses notes from an E♭ Dorian mode which is a half step above the D Dorian mode usually used on this chord?

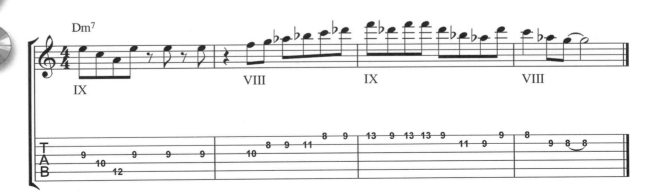

30

RING MODULATOR EFFECT:

Get an alligator clip (small) and clip it on the 6th string (or the 5th or 4th) an inch or so from the bridge. This will create all kinds of strange overtones similar to the sound made by a ring modulator. Ring modulators are mostly used in synthesizers. They combine two waveforms, and output the sum and difference between the two. This process of ring modulation, which is also amplitude modulation, produces a signal rich in overtones, suitable for producing bell-like or otherwise metallic sounds. Try using this sound with a looping device, play a few notes and then loop them while you play along. Weird and wild!

31

In this Jazz lick I've used 4 part arpeggios over the F^7 chord. After the opening Fm^7 arpeggio (inferring #9) you go to a Cm^7 then Gm^7 arpeggio followed by a chromatic resolution to the major 7th note on the $B^\flat$ chord.

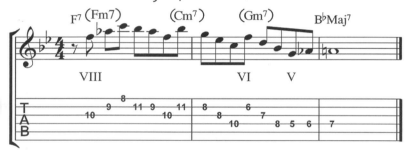

32

The minor^9 chord can be substituted for a minor^7 chord if it's a Im, IIm, IVm, Vm, VIm or any minor^7 chord with a nondiatonic root.
The minor^6 chord usually follows the IV major chord in a progression. For example, in the key of C, Fmaj^7 to Fm^6. It can also be a minor$^{7(\flat5)}$ or a dom^9 chord. Many chords have more than one name depending on where you think the root is located. Below, the ( ) parenthesis is for the root of a min$^{7\flat5}$ chord and the X is for the root of a dom^9 chord. You'll find that many multi-named chords don't have roots in them, that's how they can function as different types of chords.

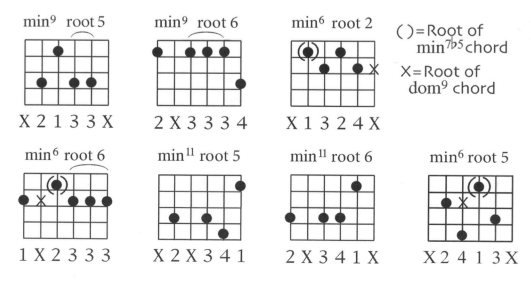

An interesting chromatic lick taken from the pedal steel. It's fairly easy to play on that instrument, not so on guitar! Remember, only bend on the 2nd string, the notes on the 1st string are not bent. Make the bends accurate and make sure you can hear each pitch. Pay attention to the rests, don't let the notes on different strings ring into each other until the 3rd measure.

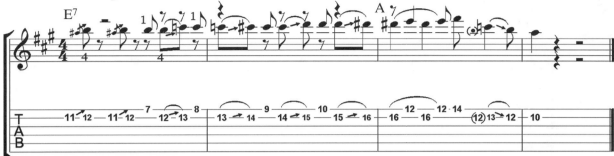

This is a similar lick, without bends, using half steps between strings.

use reverse alternate picking

On the recording I added an ending using the old cliche major pentatonic lick but tried to make it more interesting by modulating up in half steps each octave of the 3 octave lick. It'll wake up the audience, assuming they're listening. ☺

This nicely shaped Jazz lick uses 4 part chord arpeggios, instead of the usual 3 note triads, over the G^7 chord. It goes from Dm^7 to Am^7 to G^7.

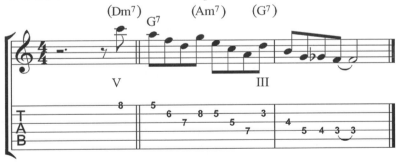

My favorite bend behind the nut Country lick. You don't think of the bottom 3 strings of the guitar as a chord, because they're not, but if you bend the 6th string up a whole step behind the nut, you get a nice major triad and the bend is the classic 2 to 3 Country lick.

natural harmonics

36

A Rockabilly lick using pull-offs to make it sound like you're doing more than you are. Once you get it going you'd probably keep playing licks like this throughout the solo.

The other example is harder because it's difficult to make those double stop pull-offs sound nice and clear. You might try sliding the finger from the 8th to the 7th fret instead of using a pull-off. It will make it a little easier.

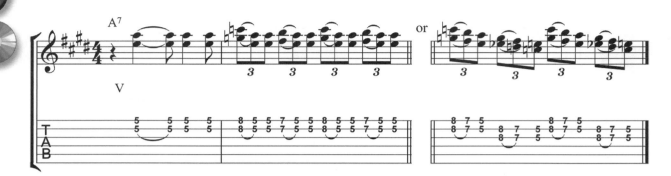

37

This is truly a Jazz lick created *on* the guitar. What I mean by that is, you just play the first 4 notes and then move that shape across the strings from high to low and you're done. If you play it fast enough it will sound good. It doesn't matter if these notes fit the chord or not. The constant structure type of fingering makes it all OK. It's fun and you'll sound cool doing it. As with all licks like this, just make sure you resolve the last note to a chord tone and you're home free.

38

The concept is called "theme and variations." This Jazz example takes the first 3 notes and uses them as the theme. Then it changes them melodically to fit the chords as they change. The rhythmic change to quarter note triplets is a variation of the theme.

39

This double bend on the top 2 strings will work in Country, Pop and Jazz and is a hard one. The high note goes up a major second (2 half steps) while the lower note goes up a minor third (3 half steps). Drag it out a bit so everyone can hear how far you're actually bending. Your first string should be gauge .009 for this to be a little easier but if you're feeling strong, you can do it with a .010 or maybe even an .011. The note in parenthesis is a "ghost" note. Played but hardly heard, more inferred.

40

Here's a hot Bluegrass style lick. This one does some nice things over the A chord. The last two measures are particularly cool. That's the kind of phrase you should take out of this example and learn in different octaves, other keys and with different fingerings.

41

Sometimes during your solo, you want to make the sound a bit bigger. Most players will start playing a mini chord solo. Usually just 3 notes at a time. Kind of a comping approach to an improvised solo. This Jazz lick uses a constant structure shape and moves it down the neck in intervals of a minor third. Notice how the notes change function with each new position. What started out as (from the bottom up) 5, ♭9 and ♯11 turns into 3, ♭7 and ♯9, then it becomes ♭9, 5 and 1 and finally ♭7, 3 and 13 before resolving to the Cmaj⁷ chord.

Arpeggiating an E major triad over an Am⁷ chord gives you a cool sounding min/maj⁷ Jazz lick. It's a sound that shows up a lot so practice thinking a perfect fifth away from whatever min⁷ chord you see and play that major triad arpeggio.

OCTAVE DISPLACEMENT:

If you want to stop playing the same worn out lines, try octave displacement. It'll make even a tired old major scale sound new and exciting. The concept is simple enough, just take a regular melody (in this case a C major scale) and mix up the octaves that the pitches are in. You should keep the order of the notes the same as the original, just not in the same octave.

Example 1 is a C scale...bor-ing!

Example 2 displaces the notes staying in second position. No matter how you do this, the resulting fingering will always be complicated. There are too many big leaps to have it come out smooth. But, nobody said it was going to be easy when you signed up!

Example 3 uses a descending major scale and stretches the pattern over a wider range making it sound wilder and even harder to finger.

See ex. 227 for my favorite displacement lick. It *will* get you noticed when you play it!

This 50's style Rock ballad has been heard in thousands of songs from *Sleep Walk* to *Surfer Girl* to the Beatles *This Boy*. I've included most of the common variations. It may start as arpeggios and go to full strumming later, or it may be arpeggios for the whole song, or strumming for the whole song. The arpeggios may or may not be muffled with the palm of the picking hand. The chord on the first beat of measure 5 is usually allowed to ring out, then put a separation between each eighth note triplet. In measure 7, you may want to separate each eighth note in the triplet as a change of pace from all the ringing chords. The addition of a little slapback echo will make this style sound more authentic.

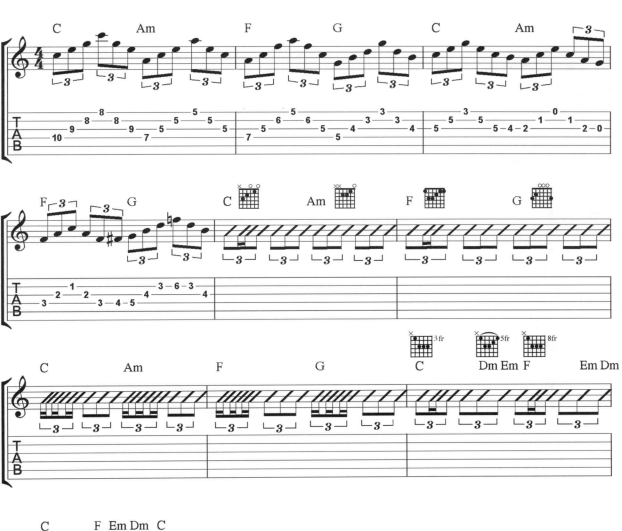

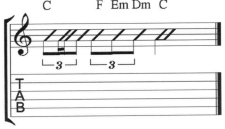

Music is the medicine of the breaking heart.

45

Nothing too unusual about this Jazz lick, just a nice C⁷ arpeggio in thirds leading you up to the 6th on the F chord resolving to the 5th.

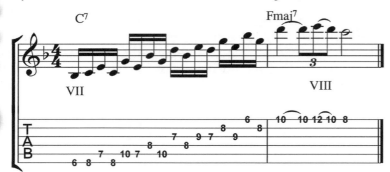

46

A Rock/Fusion example that uses parallel triad arpeggios to create an interesting sound. The first measure has a G major triad and the example ends with a 3 note lick played in leaps of ascending minor 3rds. Once again, the ear doesn't mind all the questionable notes being played as long as there's a strong resolution at the end.

47

Here is an extended example using the same pedal steel bend as ex. 14 but with a descending chromatic line in the bass. These are the kind of licks you need to analyze. The second measure is a very nice lick on a D⁷ chord. Remember it the next time you come across a dom⁷ chord in a song.

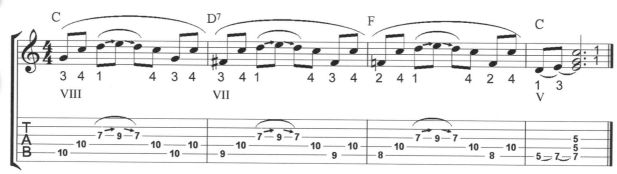

48 Using a repetitive figure whose high note is changed to suit the chord of the moment makes this Jazz lick stand out.

49 The Blues scale or minor pentatonic is made from the root, flat 3rd, 4th, 5th and flat 7th of a major scale. It is exactly the same as the major pentatonic scale. It all depends on where you think the root of the scale is. This example is a C Blues scale (C minor pentatonic) but it could be called an E♭ major pentatonic scale as well. The second example adds other scale and chromatic notes; the 2nd, optional natural 3rd, flat 5th and 6th. This makes for a more melodic Blues scale.

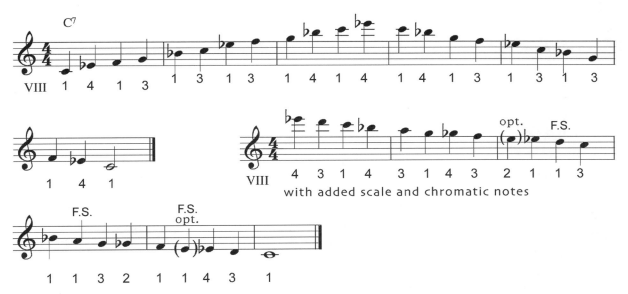

with added scale and chromatic notes

50 This Country lick shows 3 ways of playing over a dominant 7th chord using bends. You can use this going from the V chord to the I chord or from the I⁷ going to the IV chord. Use your pick and your middle finger on this example. Snap the first string with the middle finger to get a funkier sound. Fretting hand fingerings appear under the notes.

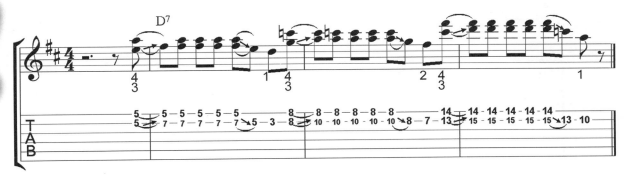

51 Here's a pretty lick with an extra "overbend." This one can be used in a Pop ballad or slow Funk kind of tune. Play a grace note bend from A to B then bend it further up to C. Release the C to A and pull-off the A to G all in one continuous, smooth movement.

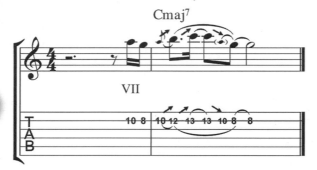

52 This Country ending lick uses a spread or open voicing for the A chord (see ex. 76 for more). The bend goes against the grain because the lower strings would get in the way if you tried to bend it in the usual direction. If you have any kind of floating vibrato system on your guitar you'll hear the low A string go flat as you bend up the 3rd string. To avoid this, either use a guitar without a whammy bar, tighten up the springs as far as they'll go or put a block of wood behind the Floyd Rose type vibrato system to lock it down.

53 Another way of playing on a diminished chord is to use a harmonic minor scale a half step above the chord's name. This will work in many situations. In this example, it's actually the most correct way to treat the chord. Remember the rule of thumb, "take the new notes (notes that aren't in the key) from the chord and add them to the key you're in at the moment, the result will always be the right scale, even if you have no idea what it is." The C#dim[7] chord has a C# and a Bb in it. Add those pitches to your C major scale and the result is a D harmonic minor scale. It doesn't matter if you know that, only that you play the right notes.

54 I've always marveled at the violin section in those pop tunes when they would play a really fast scale lick building up to the chorus or into a bridge. Well, here's one that takes you from C⁷ to F, *if* you can play it fast enough to sound authentic. Otherwise, it's just a scale exercise with a few chromatics thrown in.

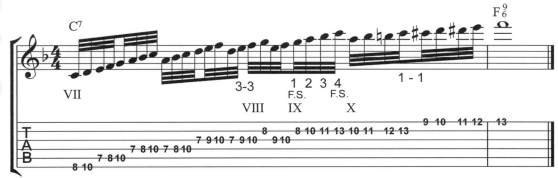

55 This Country example is the original yodel lick. You can expand upon it and get a lot of good licks in 6ths. It also works well in Blues.
(See ex. 17, 21, 61, 65, 103, 234 and 271 for more sixth licks).

56 Here is a very easy way to play a whole tone scale (see ex. 3 for more).

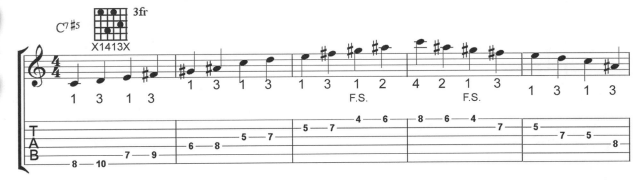

This Jazz or Western Swing lick uses a repetitive pattern made from a chromatic approach to the low note, then an octave leap to the high note. Since it's a 3 note phrase, it displaces itself nicely throughout the measures.
Be careful with your picking, those string skips can be pretty hard at a fast tempo.

In this variation, you start right on the beat instead of using pickup notes. It changes the whole feel of the lick.
Anytime you can take a phrase and start it a quarter beat or an eighth beat before or after it usually starts, you'll create an entirely new sounding lick.

In this last variation, triplets are used. The phrase is no longer displaced because each 3 note pattern starts right on the beat, but the triplet makes it sound interesting by itself.

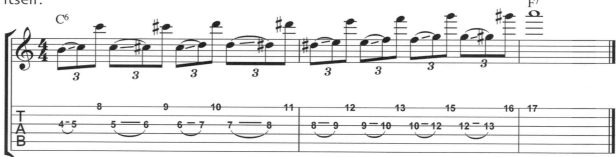

Another all purpose pattern that works as well in Jazz as it does in Blues or Country. It uses the concept of tension resolution. That means that tension 9 wants to resolve down to the root, the 7th goes up to the root, the 6th down to the 5th and the 4th down to the 3rd. The exception being in Country music where the 9 (or 2) always goes up to the 3rd.

59 Dominant 7th chords are built from the root, 3rd, 5th and flat 7th of a major scale. They are found diatonically as the V chord. They are used in place of plain major chords in Blues and Rock.

dom⁷ root 5

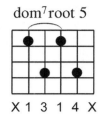

X 1 3 1 4 X

dom⁷ root 6

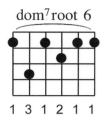

1 3 1 2 1 1

dom⁷ root 5 or 2

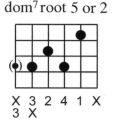

X 3 2 4 1 X
3 X

60 What do you play when those nasty diminished chords show up? It gets old real fast running up the neck playing the same diminished chord through its inversions. This example does use the ascending diminished chord, *but*, a melody is added to give it a much hipper sound. Available tensions are always a whole step above a chord tone on a diminished chord. This lick shows off those tensions and then resolves them nicely to the F major chord. Don't forget, you don't have to use the whole lick every time you see a diminished chord. Use the first 2 or 3 beats and as with all the unique licks you're learning in this book, "Don't overuse them!" that's the surest way to kill their effectiveness. In this example, C⁷♭⁹ is the same as Gdim⁷ (see ex. 240 for more).

61 Using 6ths is a common technique in Country music, but this time you're bending into the low note of each 6th. The fingering remains the same throughout the example, but the bends change between half step and whole step bends. Your 4th finger stays on the high note and your 2nd finger on the low note. The natural harmonic lick at the end is another great pedal steel lick. Bend the fifth string up a whole step behind the nut.

SWEEP ARPEGGIOS:

OK, for all you Metal guys, here's a sweep example. My friend and fellow Berklee faculty member, Joe Stump, gave me this one. On the recording, I asked Joe to come in and play it for you. Let's face it, even I can't play *everything,* although I like to think I can. Sure, I can play this, but not at *Warp 7* like Joe can! The picking pattern is called (strangely enough) arpeggio picking, which means you play a downstroke on every new string and when there's more than one note on a string you revert to alternate picking. Follow the picking indications in the example. Good luck!
On the recording, Joe is tuned down a half step.

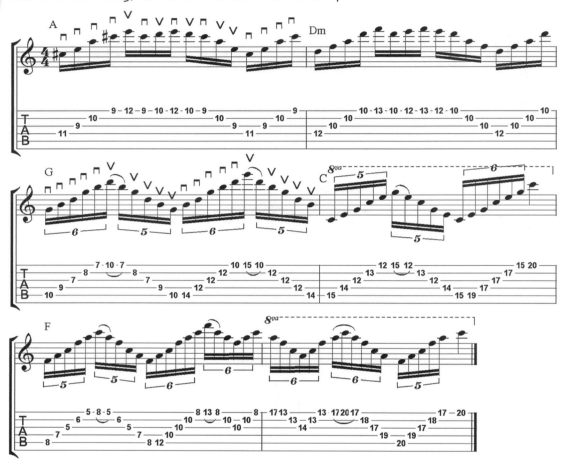

In this Jazz lick, I'm using a repetitive pattern of 3 notes, each one starting on the next note in the scale and the whole pattern starts on the raised 7th degree of the Em chord. Sure, it's a chromatic approach, but on a minor chord it sounds more like a natural 7th against the chord. Adding the natural 7th note into a min7 chord scale can sound pretty good as long as you're careful with its resolution.

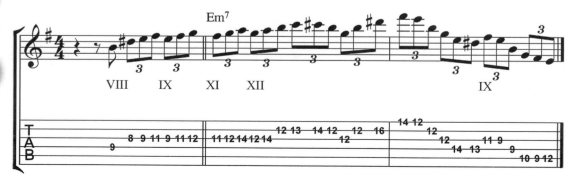

MAJOR SCALE FINGERINGS:

Here are 3 basic major scale fingerings shown in second position (the first finger is placed over the second fret). These are "moveable" scale fingerings because they contain no open strings. These three are standard fingerings that should help you get familiar with the basic scale shapes. The F.S. stands for "finger stretch." Keep your fingers positioned over the frets and stretch your first finger to get the note. The scale fingering types are named to make it easier to remember which fingering is which. Type 1 has a first finger stretch and type 1a has two first finger stretches. Type 2 has no stretches. All the scale fingerings shown in this book should be memorized and practiced in all keys and all positions.

type 1   C major

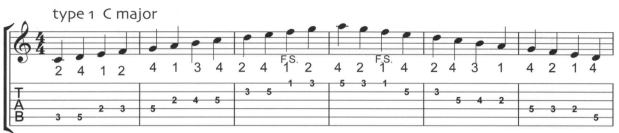

type 1a   F major

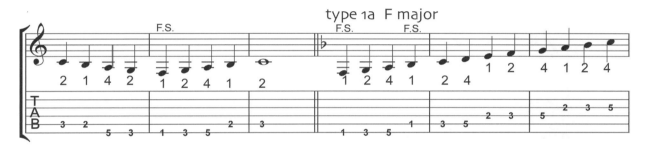

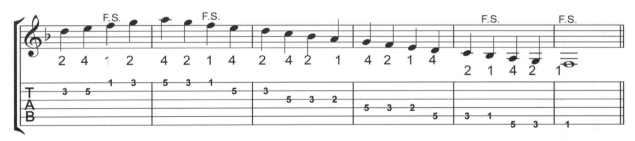

type 2   G major

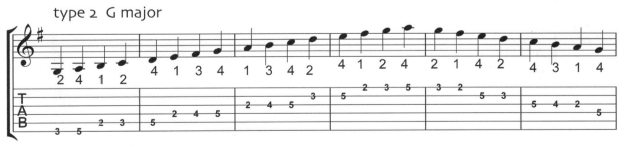

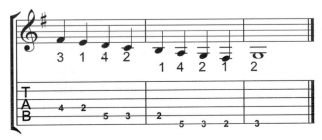

MEMORIZE THIS RULE:
To change a major scale into...
1. Melodic minor, flat the 3rd.
2. Harmonic minor, flat the 3rd and the 6th.
3. Natural minor, flat the 3rd, 6th and 7th.

65

A Country exercise in sixths, sliding while hammering and overall smoothness. The grace note into the first beat, and almost all grace notes going to a note of a quarter beat or longer, should be stretched out and played "when you get around to it," not as rigidly as legit grace notes. More precisely, that means you should almost double the length of the grace note. The pick up notes use a combination of sliding and hammering. Keep your first finger barred across the top 3 strings even when you add your second finger to it. In order to help the sustain of the quarter notes sliding down on beats 3 and 4 in the first measure to beat one in the second measure, press down as hard as you can on the strings. Using a compressor/limiter will help as well.

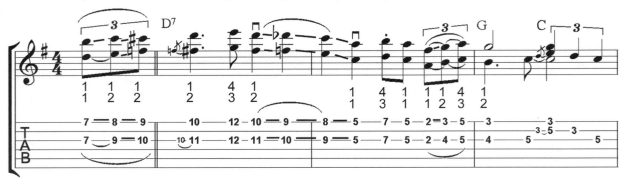

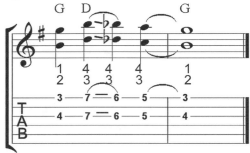

66

When you're jamming on a Dorian tune and getting tired of the same old Blues licks or Dorian scales, throw in this Jazz phrase to spice things up a bit. It's one of my favorites because it has such a nice melodic shape to it.

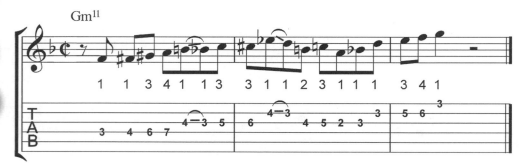

67

Another example of playing in an odd time signature. This time it's 9/8. It can be broken up into a lot of different rhythms but usually it's groups of 2 and 3. The first 3 measures would be counted 1-2, 1-2, 1-2, 1-2-3 and the last measure would be 1-2-3-, 1-2-3, 1-2-3. The accents correspond to the way you count it.

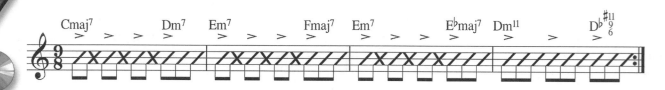

Combining 2 major pentatonic scales can give you a new sound. This lick works in Jazz as well as Blues and Country. It starts with F major pentatonic and finishes with C major pentatonic. Playing the scale in fourths also adds to the beauty of this phrase. Anytime you find something like this that sounds so nice on the Fmaj^7 chord, try it on other chords as well. For example, on the recording, I play this example as written over an Fmaj^7 chord and then over a Dm^7 chord, a B$^\flat$maj^7 and a C^{9}sus^4 chord. Instead of waiting for an opportunity to use this as written, you can have more choices if you learn how these notes relate to different chords. It will expand the usefulness of your licks.

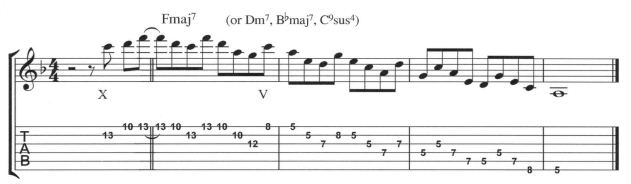

The chromatic scale, simply made up of half steps, has some good uses. In this example, it's played as triplets over a diminished chord. Each new set of triplets starts on a chord tone of the diminshed chord. If you play it as sixteenth notes, each new group starts on a chord tone of an augmented chord. Most often, you'll play the scale in smaller pieces and generally it's just a way to get from one note to another in the smoothest way possible. Chromaticism is a very important part of Jazz phrasing and you'll find it in just about every other style as well.

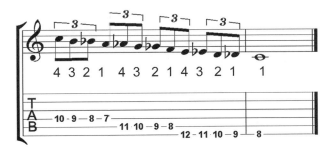

70 Pop Rock rhythms are regular strumming patterns without any fancy stuff thrown in. Any song that fits into the category of pleasant, nonoffensive, easy listening, light Rock, will accept rhythms like these. The (>) accents are there to remind you to give the **X**'s a little extra whack to bring their volume up to match the regular chord sound. You can use open position chords if you like to make this even more folksy.

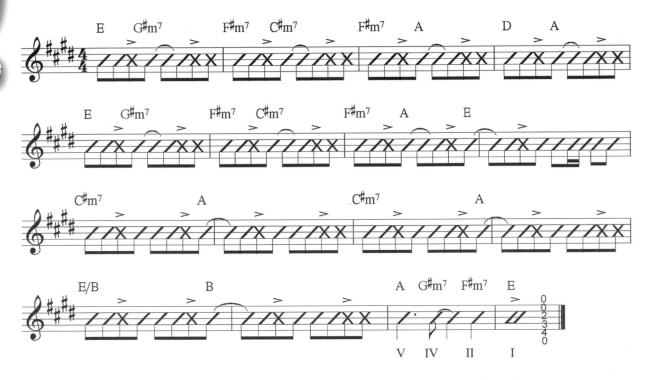

71 The harmonic major scale is an odd one, it is only used on a few chords. Its most common use is on a dom$^{7(13\flat 9)}$. As I mentioned in ex. 148, the chord tells you to only add an A$^\flat$ to your C scale. What you end up with is a C harmonic major scale. Modally, it would be called G Mixolydian $\flat$2. Here it's shown in second position but as with all the scales you learn, you must know them in all positions. Remember, the harmonic major scale is just a major scale with a flat 6th degree. The chord scale rule is this, when you see a dom$^{7(13\flat 9)}$, play the harmonic major scale up a fourth from the chord name. In the Stevie Wonder song, *The Sunshine of My Life,* the 4th chord (in the key of C) is A$^{7(13\flat 9)}$ which would take a D harmonic major scale.

72 The use of the interval of a fourth lined up on the same frets make this Jazz lick fairly easy to play and creates a very cool sound. The Fm⁷ arpeggio against the Am⁷ chord may seem a bit weird but players like Miles Davis and Dizzy Gillespie used arpeggios a minor 6th away to add spice and surprise to their solos.

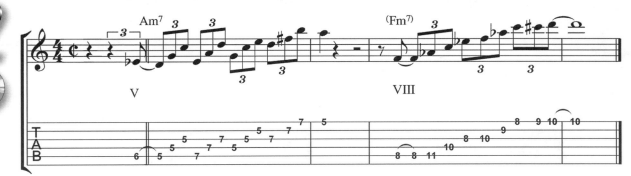

73 Take a 6 note pattern like the first 6 notes of this Jazz lick and move that same pattern around changing the notes to fit the chord but keeping the basic shape. On the Em⁷ chord the lick starts on the ♭7 and incorporates the 5th, 3rd and the root. On the Dm⁷, it starts on the 11th then goes to the 9th, ♭7th, 5th and ♭3rd. On the G⁷ it uses basic chord tones and is followed by a big 2 octave Cmaj⁷ arpeggio.

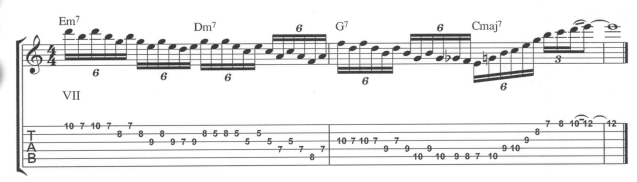

74 There may not be many times when you're called upon to create the sound of a snare drum, but it's always good to be prepared!

THE SNARE DRUM

Drag the 6th string off the fretboard towards the back of the neck until it buzzes like a snare drum.

WORDS OF WISDOM:
When I'm on a gig and someone calls a Latin tune or a Bossa Nova that I don't know (which can happen fairly often) I go into my percussion bag of tricks and play sounds like the ones found in ex. 86 and 168. I not only cover my butt, while I listen to the piano player and try to hear the changes in hopes of playing them the second time through, but everyone thinks I'm so cool adding all these wonderful sounds to help make the band sound better. Heh heh!

75

This "Memphis Vamp" is so called because the first time it showed up in a pop tune was a song called *Memphis*, written by Chuck Berry and made famous by Johnny Rivers. It can be used in tons of other styles as well. It sounds great in Rock or Blues. In this example, the dotted eighth and sixteenth rhythm means to use a swing or shuffle feel. Use the A chord box whenever an A chord is written, the D box for the D chord and the A⁷ box when you see A⁷ written.

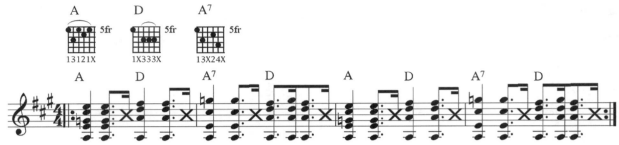

76

SPREAD VOICINGS:

Take a close voiced triad (3 notes stacked as close together as possible) and move the middle note up an octave (or down an octave). The result is what's called an open or spread voicing. These have a nice big sound and are useful in chord solos, comping and when trying to fake classical guitar music.

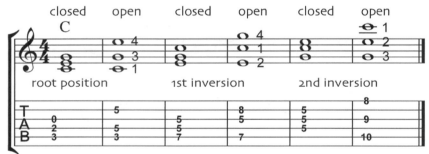

77

A dom⁷⁽♯⁹⁾ or dom⁷⁽⁺⁹⁾ chord is built from the root, 3rd, 5th, flat 7th and sharp 9th of a major scale. It's used very often in Rock and Funk and almost as much in Jazz and Blues. To a lot of guitarists, it's known as "The Hendrix Chord" because of the tune *Purple Haze*. You can't just throw a ♯9 onto a I⁷, II⁷, IV⁷ or V⁷ chord because it's an altered tension, that is, one that doesn't occur naturally in the chord scale. If it's a III⁷, VI⁷ or VII⁷ it can be considered an available tension. But, in a lot of Rock, Blues and Funk tunes, it's used on the I, IV and V chords anyway to get that nasty sound.

dom⁷♯⁹ root 5

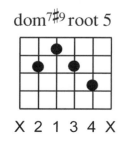

X 2 1 3 4 X

dom⁷♯⁹ root 6

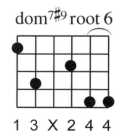

1 3 X 2 4 4

dom⁷♯⁹ root 5

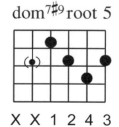

X X 1 2 4 3

dom⁷♯⁹ root 6

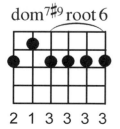

2 1 3 3 3 3

Music is what feelings sound like.

78

An interesting constant structure Jazz lick. The first shape creates the tensions 13, #11, 9 and b7 over the G7 chord, but when you move it down a fret, they become tensions #9, 1, b13 and 3 over the C7 chord. I find this example a lot easier to play when I finger-pick it. It's really hard to play fast with just a flatpick.

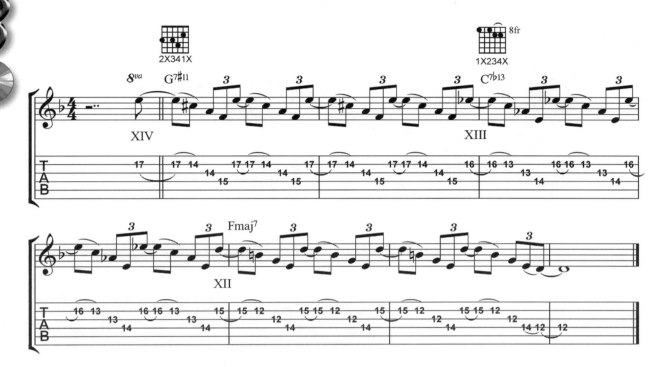

79

A Metal/Acid Rock type of rhythm guitar pattern that uses power chords (only the root, fifth and octave root are played). The third of the chord just gets in the way. Actually, with distortion, the third breaks up the chord and doesn't sound very good. The interval of a perfect fifth creates the "difference tone" of a root, an octave below the one being played, giving it that big powerful sound (see ex. 128 for more about difference tones). In measures 9 and 10, there are 4 different inversions of a sharp 9 chord. I don't think Hendrix would have done it this way, but it still sounds good. Use the thumb on your fretting hand to block the low E's in those same measures. You don't want the low E ringing into the chords.

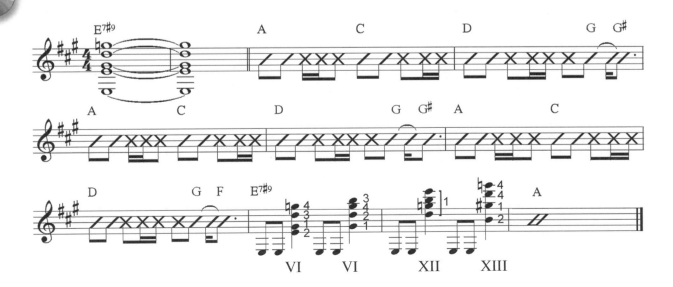

Fretting hand positon for Rock or Country or when playing the 6th string with the thumb.

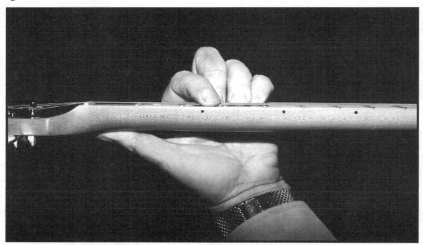

Proper fretting hand positon for "most" chord forms.

STUFF YOU SHOULD ALREADY KNOW • but in case you don't, here it is...

To figure out sharp keys, go up a half step from the last sharp to the right. In A, a key with 3 sharps, the last sharp to the right is G#, go up a half step to A, that's the key. To figure out flat keys, move back one flat to the left of the last flat on the right. In Eb, a key with 3 flats, the last flat to the right is a Ab, move back one flat to the left to get to the Eb, that's the key.

APPROACH TECHNIQUES:

I remember when I first started to listen to Jazz players, I couldn't figure out where they were getting all those notes from! I knew about scales and arpeggios but there was something else going on that I wasn't hip to. The answer was Approach Techniques, and when my teacher at the time, Larry Senibaldi, told me about them, it opened up a whole new world in my soloing. All of a sudden, I could hear what those Jazz guys were doing. What makes it even more fun is that it's pretty easy to do. You start with the notes of a chord, like the C major chord below, then you approach them in various ways. You delay getting to those chord tones by playing other notes before them. This first example is using diatonic approach notes (notes from the key). First I use "diatonic from above" which means, I play the next available note above my target note *before* I play the target note. So, before I play the C, I play a D, then an F before the E and so on.

The C chord shows you the notes you'll be approaching.
Ex. 1 is "diatonic from above."
Ex. 2 is "diatonic from below" which turns out to almost be a scale.
Ex. 3 is "diatonic from below and above" so you start with the diatonic note
    below your target note, then go to the diatonic note above your target
    note, then finally reach the target note.
Ex. 4 is "diatonic from above and below." Start above the target, then below
    the target, then play the target note.

The next 4 examples use chromatic approaches to a C triad. In the same manner as the previous examples, I start with chromatic from below, then chromatic from above, then chromatic from below and above and finally chromatic from above and below.

Some of these will sound better to you then others. That's the point. Begin making your own decisions about what sounds good to *you* and you'll start to develop your own style.

APPROACH TECHNIQUES continued:

Now we'll combine the diatonic approach with the chromatic approach. This is where it starts to get interesting. You may recognize the sound of some of these examples. They're used a lot, particularly in Jazz. Number 1 is diatonic from below with chromatic from above. Number 2 is chromatic from below with diatonic from above. Number 3 is chromatic from above with diatonic from below and number 4, one of the most common, is diatonic from above with chromatic from below.

The rhythms in this example are certainly not the only rhythms you can use with these techniques. Try starting with the root and going up from there. Try displacing everything by an eighth note or make them triplets. The more ways you change them around, the better they start to sound.

Here are some other approach technique possibilities. Number 1 is double chromatic from below. Number 2 is double chromatic from above. Number 3 is triple chromatic from below and number 4 is triple chromatic from above. I think you're starting to get the idea. You can approach any note from any other note. But if you make a pattern out of it, it sounds like some fancy new lick when it's really just a simple approach technique.

Way back in 1966, our band, The Uncalled Four, was going to play at The Cafe Wha? in Greenwich Village, New York City. This was a really big deal for us. Newcomers (at the time) Bob Dylan, Jimi Hendrix, Bruce Springsteen, Peter, Paul & Mary, as well as comedians Richard Pryor and Bill Cosby all got their start there and of course we were all hoping to become the next Beatles. None of us had long hair at the time so we decided to buy wigs! We went to Sears, bought wigs and brought them to a local hair salon to have them cut into styles more appropriate for a 60's Rock band.

The gig went great, we all played well and the crowd seemed to like us a lot. The funny part was, it was hot as hell in there and I was sweating like crazy. The sweat was literally pouring down my face and all over my guitar, BUT, my hair was perfect! It stayed dry and in place for the whole night.
Do you think anyboby noticed? ☺
(I'm the guy with the shades on)

85

50's and 60's style Rock lead guitar, in the style of Chuck Berry, has a driving, primitive quality to it. Use downstrokes on everything but the triplets at the end. If you only played the licks in measures 3 and 10, you could get through an entire solo. A little bit of slapback echo and a touch of natural amp distortion will make your sound even more authentic.

PERCUSSION EFFECTS:

My favorite percussive sound on the guitar is the Bongo/Conga sound. It can be used in many styles from Latin to Rock to Jazz. Experiment with pickup combinations to get the most realistic sound. The rhythm shown in the first example is so cliche I'm amazed how often you hear it. With minor variations, it's played in every single tune containing congas I've ever heard. See ex. 74 and 168 for more.

Hold the strings dead around the 5th fret, tap around the 15th fret
High pitch = top 3 strings, lower pitch = bottom 3 strings.

Stems down notes are fretting hand slaps with the 2nd finger.

This is the classic "Train Rhythm," so called because the drummer plays an accented roll on the snare drum that sounds like a train rolling down the tracks. Thousands of Country songs have been written around this groove. There are plenty of variations to this rhythm, but this is the basic one you *must* know. Muffle the bass strings and use a thumbpick to get a good solid attack on those low strings. One common variation is to hammer-on from G♮ to G♯ on each E chord in the manner of a grace note. Slapback echo set for an eighth beat after the attack is a must for this to sound authentic.

Muffle the bottom 3 strings.

I call this my all-purpose-finger-picking-pattern. You can use it for almost any Folk, Country, Ragtime or Pop ballad tune. Just remember the picking hand pattern of thumb-1-thumb-2. That's all there is to it. With a few variations, it can fit in a multitude of styles. See ex. 161 and 199 for more.

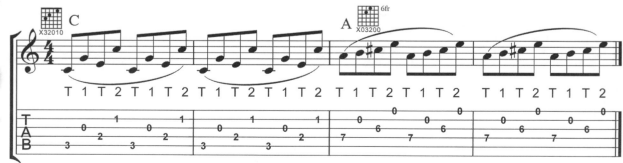

8

9

The photo shows you how to bend a note behind the nut while also bending a note in the usual manner. It will produce a sound similar to a "B-Bender" (see ex. 248 and 249). That is the only other way you could bend a note on the 3rd string and have another bend on the 2nd string.

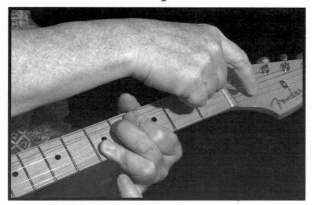

9

0

This C major pentatonic lick has a different sound to it because of the hammers and slides (slurs and glisses). Make sure you give each note its proper time value before leaving it to go on to the next one.

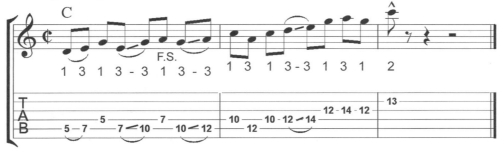

9

1

Here are 2 variations of one of the most used Blues licks of all time. You can't listen to someone play a blues solo without hearing this lick in one form or another. The concept is to start on the root, then run a chromatic scale from the flat 3rd to the 5th, then jump down to the root again. In this example it's shown in 2 different octaves.

In the next example, when you play the A♭, you start bending up to each note from there without ever leaving the 9th fret. It's a great emotional way to play the lick but difficult to play in tune with all those half step bends. Use it anywhere you want during the 12 bar form. Since you're bending farther than usual, make a big deal out of it. Make a face like it hurts and lift your guitar neck upwards...show biz!

92

A flashy sounding lick you can use in a lot of situations. Remember to try to have all the pull-off notes sound at the same volume as the picked ones. The Nashville cats use this technique a lot.

93

A constant structure Jazz lick. Take a major triad starting on the third of the A chord (C# or D♭) and run it up the neck in half steps making sure to resolve it to a strong note. In this case, the last C to C# resolves it to the 3rd of the A chord.
Does it make any musical or harmonic sense? No. But it doesn't have to. The listener is drawn upwards with the sound and because it's a constant structure, we don't mind all the wrong notes going by. It's like we're just along for the ride and waiting to see where it ends.

94

MAJOR 7 CHORDS:

Major 7th chords are built from the root, 3rd, 5th and 7th degrees of a major scale. Typically the I and IV chords of a key. Remember, when it says root 5, the name of the chord is on the fifth string. If the first form was on the 5th fret, it would be a Dmaj⁷ chord.

major⁷ root 5   major⁷ root 6   major⁷ root 4   major⁷ root 6   major⁷ root 5

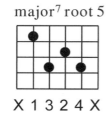   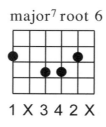   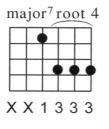   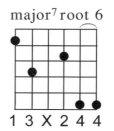   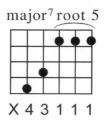

X 1 3 2 4 X   1 X 3 4 2 X   X X 1 3 3 3   1 3 X 2 4 4   X 4 3 1 1 1

95

Another one of those "guitar" licks that are easy to play because of the repetitive fingering. It's a good Rock lick, Country lick or even a Jazz lick depending on what chord you play it over. I have it written over an Am^7 chord, but it will work just as well over an A^7, C^6, $Fmaj^7$, Em^9 and others. Keep experimenting and see what other chords a particular lick might sound good over. You can pick this with alternate picking or arpeggio picking (downstroke on each new string). Give the next to last note, C, a little quarter step squeeze for color.

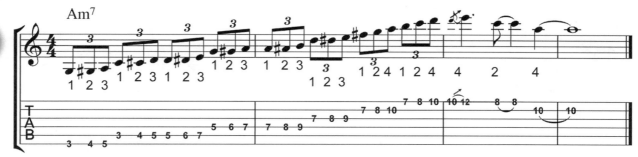

96

Bending behind the nut can create some nice sounding licks. In the first measure it's a G chord with the bend adding sus^4. The third measure uses a double bend (2nd and 3rd finger suggested). Be careful with your intonation. This technique works well in many styles. Also, if your string doesn't come back in tune after a bend behind the nut, it's because the string is getting caught in the nut. To fix it, either buy a graphite nut, spray some graphite spray in the cut slots in the nut, or just rub some pencil lead in there (it's graphite, not lead).

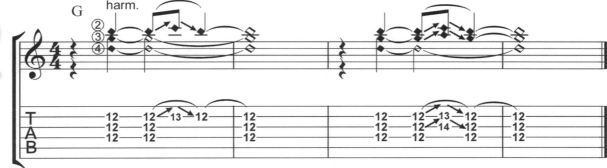

97

In a lot of Fusion solos, you'll hear a single phrase repeated and moved chromatically up or down (usually up). It helps if it's rhythmically unusual as well. This lick is a 6 beat pattern that repeats every 3 bars. There's no chord listed because it really doesn't matter (on the recording I played it over an $E^{7\#9}$). Like most parallel licks, start on a chord tone and end on a chord tone and what happens between them can be almost anything.

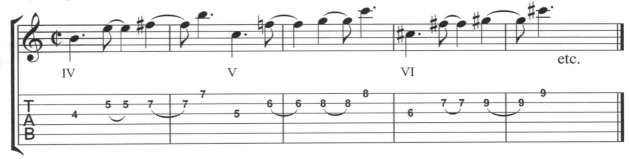

BASIC ROCK RHYTHM GUITAR:

Alternate picking throughout. Keep an even tempo and try playing the entire page without stopping. The B♭m⁷ chord is a chromatic approach to the Bm⁷. You can use chromatic approaches anywhere you want to make the rhythms more interesting. Make sure you hit the "X" with more force than the regular chords to give it that snare drum attack. You are, after all, mimicking the drummer's beat.

COMPLEX ROCK RHYTHM GUITAR:

These rhythms are the same as the Basic Rock Rhythm Guitar rhythms on the previous page. The only difference is the addition of sixteenth notes. Now the eighth notes are all down strokes and the sixteenths are alternate.

INSTANT CHORD MELODIES:

There's a big difference between chord melodies and chord solos. A chord melody is a simple harmonization of a melody. A chord solo uses reharmonizations, bass lines, filler licks and much more. It's a composition, something you sit down and work out until it's finished. A chord melody should be able to be improvised on the spot.

In order to be able to create a chord melody, you'll need the following:

1. A fairly large amount of chord forms. At least 3 fingerings for every type of chord (if you learn all the chords in this book, you'll have enough).

2. Knowledge of what note (pitch name and function of the chord) is on the top of each of those chord forms.

3. The ability to transpose a tune to a guitar friendly key. Most standard tunes are written in flat keys, it's better for horn players and piano players. Unfortunately, guitar just doesn't "sing" in keys like E♭. Remember, you're doing these solos to be played accapella (by yourself without a band) so transpose them to a key like C, G, A, E or D so you can use open strings now and then. Don't forget, it's a *guitar* solo, not a piano solo, and a big old E chord sounds a lot fatter than an E♭ chord.

Here's a tune that used to be in B♭. I dropped it down to A to make it more guitar friendly. All you have to do is play a chord with the right melody note each time a new chord shows up. These chords are mostly occurring 2 beats apart so you only need to play a new voicing when the chord changes. You don't have to (and it sounds better if you don't) put a chord on every single melody note.

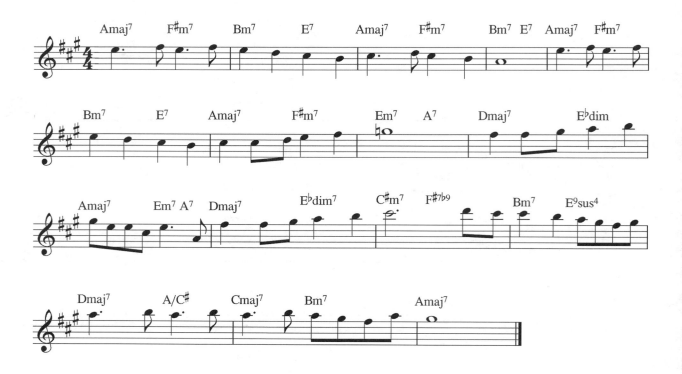

INSTANT CHORD MELODY continued

Here's the finished chord melody. These are all basic chord forms and it should be fairly easy to play. The hardest part of all chord melodies or chord solos is changing from one voicing to the next without leaving any holes in the sound. The melody must sound the same as it would if it were played without the harmonization. Record yourself playing this and listen for any gaps in the sound. Always strive for the smoothest transition possible. Another way to think about it is, hold on to one chord until the last possible millisecond before you have to move to the next chord. Try different picking techniques to vary the sound of the solo. You could play it with a pick or with fingers only. My favorite way is with a pick but as you strum a chord, your second finger plays the melody note. Timing is critical with this technique. Your second finger must pick the melody note as the pick reaches the end of its strum.

101

The melodic minor scale is nothing more than a major scale with a flat 3rd degree. Here is D melodic minor used over a G⁷ chord which changes it into a G Lydian ♭7 mode. From G, you would build a major scale with a sharp 4th and a flat 7th degree (compared to G major). From D you would just flat the 3rd of a D major scale. In traditional classical music, the melodic minor scale changes depending on whether it's going up or down. It goes up melodic minor and comes down natural minor. Since that would be useless in Jazz, they just changed the name from traditional melodic minor to real melodic minor or Jazz minor. Be sure to practice changing all your major scales into melodic minor by just flatting the 3rd degree.

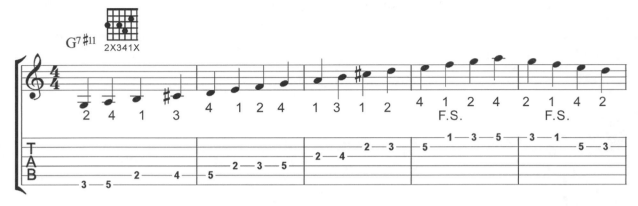

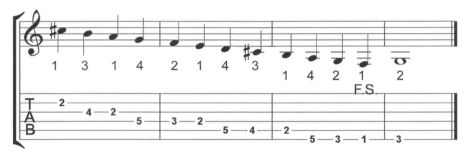

102

Play this funky Country lick fast! I find it easier to play with just fingers, but you may want to try it with pick and fingers. Either way, snap the strings to get a percussive attack and if you can, put your pickups out of phase like position 2 or 4 on a 5 way toggle switch. Even though there is no Lydian to speak of in Country music, the double bend in measure 4 starts on the sharped 4th degree. Who cares! It sounds good.

103

Here is a new Country technique. It takes the regular sixths and adds a lower note an octave below the high note. Usually played in triplets, it can also be played in eighths or sixteenths. Don't let the sixth interval ring into the lower note, they must remain separate from each other to get the right sound. Use pick and finger for this one. The pick is on strings 3 and 4 with the middle finger on string 1. Keep your first finger barred across the top 3 strings thoughout the example, even when you're using the 2nd finger.

104

Refer to ex. 116 as to which dominant 7 chords take the Lydian ♭7 scale. This Jazz lick shows off that Lydian dominant sound. On the recording I used a chord progression of Cmaj⁷, F⁷ (with the written lick), Em⁷, E♭9, Dm⁷, D♭9 and Cmaj⁷. On each dominant chord I played the same written lick transposed down a whole step.

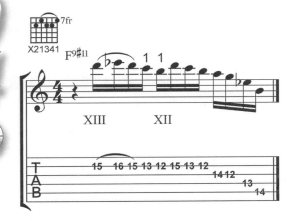

105

This Country lick uses chromatics between the 2nd and 3rd strings. Pay close attention to the rests and don't let the notes ring into each other. Start on a chord tone and end on a chord tone. You can make it fit into one measure or drag it out to cover 3 or 4. Try playing this lick in reverse as well. Mix it up, go up for a while then turn around and come down. As always, experiment, create your own versions of these licks.

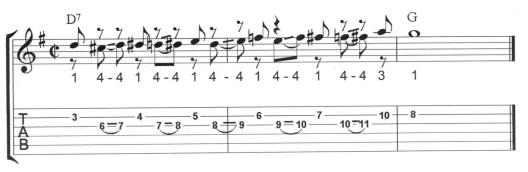

JAZZ - A BRIEF HISTORY:

Born in America, Jazz and musicals are one of the greatest cultural inventions in the United States. Jazz found a way of bridging the gap between Classical and popular music which made it assessable to a wider audience. Jazz is often called "America's Classical Music." Defined as a style of instrumental and vocal music which was Afro American in origin, there is extensive use of improvisation, performance technique that is usually above average and often uses a swing rhythm at its core. Jazz today is a mixture of almost any style imaginable and this allows it to be played and enjoyed around the world.

It all started in New Orleans, Louisiana, around the turn of the 20th century. New Orleans was an important trade center and a melting pot for a wide variety of cultures. Jazz is a blend of African Tribal, European and American music.

The new music that started in New Orleans was called "Hot Jazz." Over time, many of the musicians found their way up the Mississippi river to Chicago, Illinois. This city gave us such notable players as Louis Armstrong and Johnny Dodds.

The 30's and 40's ushered in the "Swing Era." Big Bands, large ensembles with Brass and Sax sections plus a 4 piece rhythm section, were performing at dance halls around the nation. Notable groups include those of Count Basie, Woody Herman and Benny Goodman. By that time, Jazz and popular music were thought of as the same thing.

After World War II, the Big Band era was beginning to fade out and as with all styles of music, the players started to experiment with new directions. The birth of Be Bop came mainly from 2 such innovators named Charlie Parker (sax) and Dizzy Gillespie (trumpet). They started a movement that created the framework on which all the modern Jazz of the second half of the 20th century was woven.

Today, Jazz has left the smoky old bars and is often played in the "hip" nightclubs, concert halls and festivals around the world. Jazz has evolved into a myriad of styles including avant-garde or free Jazz, smooth Jazz, Fusion, Latin Jazz and many others.

Here's a list of some of the most essential albums to listen to if you want to hear how Jazz developed: Cannonball Adderley, *Somethin' Else*, Louis Armstrong, *The Complete Hot Five & Hot Seven Recordings*, Count Basie, *The Essential Count Basie, Volumes I & II*, Sidney Bechet, *The Sidney Bechet Story*, Art Blakey, *The Best of Art Blakey and the Jazz Messengers*, Bix Beiderbecke, *Singin' the Blues, Vol. I* and *At the Jazz Band Ball, Vol. 2*, John Coltrane, *Blue Train*, Miles Davis, *Kind of Blue*, Duke Ellington, *The Duke at His Best*, Ella Fitzgerald, *Clap Hands, Here Comes Charlie*, Dizzy Gillespie, *The Complete RCA Victor Recordings*, Benny Goodman, *Ken Burns' JAZZ Series, Benny Goodman*, Coleman Hawkins, *A Retrospective 1929-1963*, Woody Herman, *The Thundering Herds 1945-1947*, Billie Holiday, *Love Songs*, Thelonious Monk, *Genius of Modern Music, Vol. 1 and Vol. 2*, Charlie Parker, *Confirmation, Best of the Verve Years*, Oscar Peterson, *The Sound of the Trio*, Django Reinhardt, *The Classic Early Recordings*, Lester Young, *The Complete Aladdin Recordings*.

Here is a list of some of the best Jazz guitarists to listen to, an incomplete list to be sure but if you start with these players, you'll have a good foundation of how it's supposed to be played: George Barnes, Billy Bauer, Ed Bickert, Lenny Breau, Kenny Burrell, Charlie Byrd, Charlie Christian, Joe Cinderella, Eddie Duran, Herb Ellis, Tal Farlow, Barry Galbraith, Hank Garland, Freddie Green, Grant Green, Tiny Grimes, Jim Hall, Al Hendrickson, Barney Kessel, Carl Kress, Eddie Lang, Mundell Lowe, Wes Montgomery, Tony Mottola, Mary Osborne, Joe Pass, Les Paul, Bucky Pizzarelli, Jimmy Raney, Django Reinhardt, Howard Roberts, Sal Salvador, Johnny Smith and George Van Eps.

Always a big hit at the clinics I do is the "Church Bell" effect. Yes, you *can* make your guitar sound like a huge bell hanging in the steeple of a church. Take your pick (heavy gauge or equivalent, sorry, none of those small Jazz picks) place it between the 5th and 4th strings. Push the pick under the 5th string with your thumb. This also brings the 4th string up and over the 5th. As the tip of the pick comes around, put it under the 6th string to keep it from unwinding the strings. Pick the twisted strings to the right of the pick. If the sound is not quite right, if it doesn't have enough overtones, slide the pick further up the neck and try different pickup combinations.

The dominant 9th chord is built from the root, 3rd, 5th, flat 7th and 9th degrees of a major scale. Adding a 9 to a dominant chord is OK if the chord is a I^7, II^7, IV^7 or V^7 chord. Using available tensions, like adding 9 or 13, will help make your rhythm playing sound fuller and more professional. The dom⁹ chord is a staple of Funk and Blues.

dom⁹ root 5   dom⁹ root 1   dom⁹ root 6

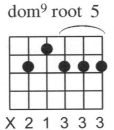 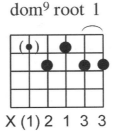 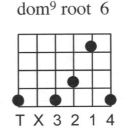

X 2 1 3 3 3   X (1) 2 1 3 3   T X 3 2 1 4

When you come across an "altered" dominant chord, the voicing must contian ♭5 or ♯5 and ♭9 or ♯9. No normal 5th or 9th degrees are allowed. It doesn't matter which you choose, as long as they're altered. Here are a few choices.

dom⁷alt (♯5/♭9) root 6   dom⁷alt (♭5/♯9) root 6   dom⁷alt (♯5/♯9) root 6   dom⁷alt (♭5/♭9) root 5

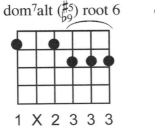 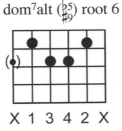 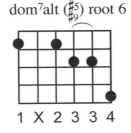 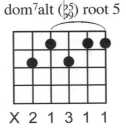

1 X 2 3 3 3   X 1 3 4 2 X   1 X 2 3 3 4   X 2 1 3 1 1

Another driving Rock example in the 50's and 60's style. I've heard players like Chuck Berry use bits and pieces of things like this but not usually quite as complicated. Once again, use all down strokes for the entire example. The little lines in front of the notes in measures 3 and 4 tell you to slide into the note from a fret or two below. Pay close attention to the slides and slurs in measures 5, 6 and 7. A little slapback echo will help and maybe just the smallest bit of amp distortion to give it some grit.

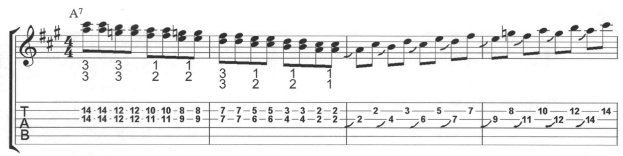

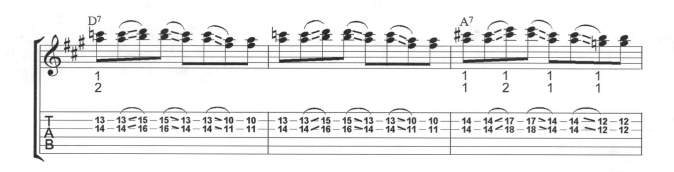

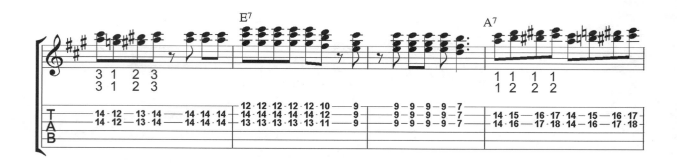

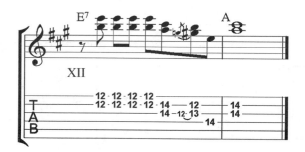

Here's a great open string lick for a Country or Bluegrass tune. Chet Atkins was a master at playing things like this. Pay close attention to the fretting hand fingerings, you will have to stretch a lot to make this work, but it sounds so good, it's worth a little pain.

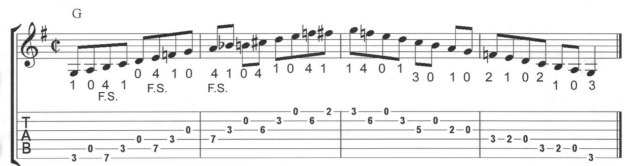

THE VIOLIN EFFECT:

Have you ever noticed how a distorted guitar sounds a lot like a violin? Well, check this out. Use a volume pedal to hide the pick attack, use the vibrato arm to get the violin style vibrato (this also allows you to keep your fingers still and not add any unwanted noise), get all the distortion you can find, add tons of reverb and play the example below. Synthesizers for strings? We don't need no stinkin' synthesizers!

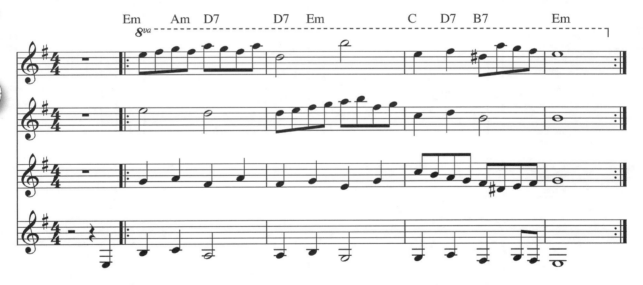

This is a fairly simple Jazz example but it's a nice way to play over a I-#Idim-II-V progression and these show up in hundreds of tunes.

PAINFUL CHORD VOICINGS:

Because of the guitar's tuning, the very pretty sound of half steps within a chord voicing is not very easy to play.

If you use open strings (see ex. 16 & 19) you can achieve some nice sounds, but what happens when open strings aren't available? You STRETCH!

These voicings are just a few of the possibilities available when you start thinking about extreme stretches. There's no easy way to play these, but you might find it a little more comfortable if you hold the guitar almost straight up towards the ceiling. That will allow your fretting hand to stretch a little easier.

Remember, many chords can have more than one name. The Cm^6 (chord 1) and the Cm^9_6 (chord 5) can also be F^9 or $Dm^{7\flat5}$, the $Amaj^9$ (chord 3) can be $F\#m^{11}$. Always try to think of other chords that might contain the same notes as the chord your playing. You'll get a lot more mileage from your voicings that way.

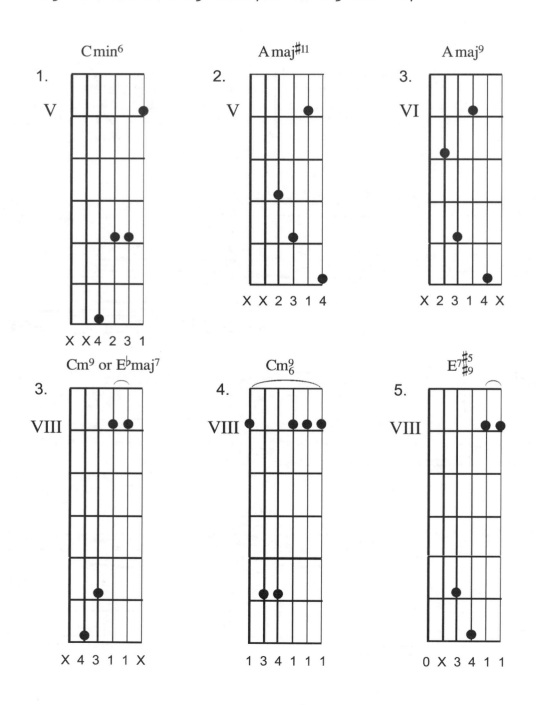

An exciting Blues lick to keep your solo moving forward. This one is almost always used in measures 11 and 12 to build intensity and kick it up a notch to get the next 12 bars off to an emotional start.

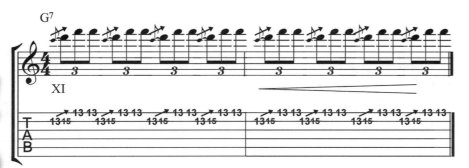

The first 2 measures are an often used "walk up" from the V chord (G) to the I chord (C). The next 5 measures are a typical "walk down" through the changes. You could stop on the F chord or continue until you're back to C. These progressions are common in Country, Folk and Pop tunes. It's really just a way of harmonizing the bass line.

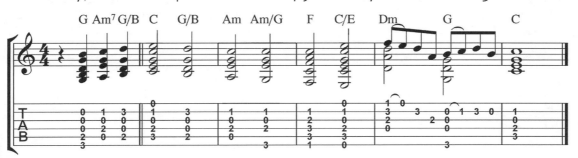

WHICH SCALE GOES WITH WHICH CHORD?

Here's the list in the key of C:
- If it's a I major chord or any other nondiatonic major chord *with* a diatonic root, Dmaj7, Emaj7 etc., play a major scale from the chord's root (Ionian mode).
- If it's the IV major chord or any other nondiatonic major chord with a *non*diatonic root, E♭maj7, A♭maj7 etc., play a major scale from the chord's 5th (Lydian mode).
- If it's a I7, II7 or V7 chord, play a major scale up a fourth (Mixolydian mode). If it's a II7 that doesn't resolve up a fourth, you can use melodic minor up a 5th (Lydian ♭7 mode).
- If it's a III7, VI7 or VII7, play a harmonic minor scale up a fourth (Mixolydian ♭2, ♭6 mode).
- If it's a nondiatonic dom7 chord with a nondiatonic root, D♭7, B♭7 etc., play a melodic minor scale from the chord's 5th (Lydian ♭7 mode).
- If it's a nondiatonic minor7 chord, play a major scale from the flat seventh of the chord (Dorian mode).
- If it's a min7♭5 chord, play a major scale up a half step (Locrian mode) or a melodic minor from the chord's 3rd (Locrian ♯2 mode).
- If it's an augmented dom7 chord, play a whole tone scale from the chord's root or a melodic minor scale up a fourth (Mixolydian ♭6 mode).
- If it's a dom7 alt chord, play a melodic minor scale up a half step (Altered or Super Locrian mode).
- If it's a dim7 chord, play a diminished scale (whole, half) from any chord tone or a harmonic minor scale up a half step (Altered ♭♭7 mode).
- If it's a dom7♭9 13, play a harmonic major scale up a fourth (Mixolydian ♭2 mode).

This is not the definitive set of rules, but it's close enough to allow you to play on any chord you come up against. The only way to get good at this is to analyze hundreds of tunes and apply these rules. Get a "Real Book" or other song book and start trying to figure out what scale goes with what chord.

117

A Bluegrass banjo style lick that uses a lot of open strings. Banjo players often play just one voicing with their fretting hand but pick in a banjo roll pattern (one finger after another) to create these very fast licks. Practice the "3 finger roll" with thumb-1-2 or pick-2-3 over and over until you can play the pattern quickly and evenly.

118

This Western Swing lick uses a scale in thirds starting on the upbeat of beat 2 in the first measure. Then, in the last two measures, a whole tone scale is used for no apparent reason. This happens a lot in Western Swing, probably because they liked the odd, jazzy sound of the scale. A whole tone scale is used on augmented chords or on dom$^{7\#5}$ chords, but "for effect" they would throw it in whenever they wanted.

119

Nothing particularly hip about this lick but it does create a very nice melodic phrase. It's well suited to Jazz, Blues and most types of ballads. It uses the approach technique of diatonic from below then diatonic from above (see ex. 81, 82, 83, 84 for more). The scale in use is the A Mixolydian mode. To make it into a lick that would work over an Amaj^7, change the key signature to A.

The concept behind this open string Country lick is to take an ordinary eighth note phrase and change it into triplets. Look at ex. 21, it starts off the same as this example but in eighth notes. When I change it to triplets, a whole new lick is created. In the last measure, hold onto the F♯ and A so that they ring for the rest of the measure.

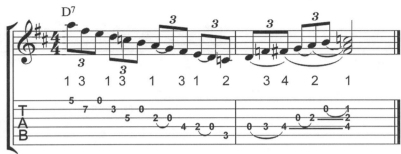

THE STRAIGHT EIGHTH and SWING EIGHTH PYRAMIDS:

In order to properly "feel" the groove of a song, you must know which pyramid is being used. As you can see, the top 3 lines of each pyramid are exactly the same. If you play whole, half or quarter notes, you can't tell which one is being used. As soon as you hear straight eighths, you know you're using the straight eighth pyramid. If you hear swing eighths (often written as dotted eighth and sixteenth) then you're using the swing eighth pyramid. This is critical when playing rhythm guitar. If you add extra strokes and percussive *chicks*, you have to know which pyramid to choose from. If you're not sure which one is being used, listen to the drummer's hi-hat cymbal. It's usually where he plays straight or swing eighths.

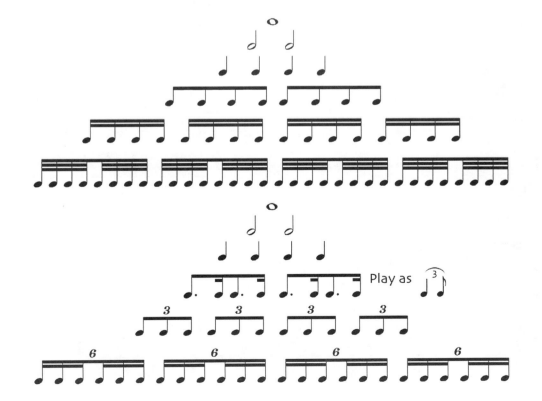

This really interesting Jazz lick is using parallel minor triads moving chromatically down the neck but then changes to major triads in the second half of the phrase. The name of each triad is shown in parenthesis.

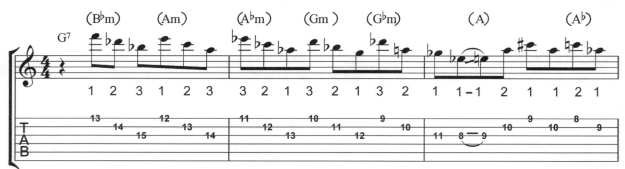

Here is another major scale fingering. This one is called type 4 because there's a 4th finger stretch in it. This fingering also becomes one of the most common major pentatonic patterns when you leave out the 4th and 7th degrees. Don't forget, the F.S. stands for finger stretch, keep your fingers in position and stretch for the G#.

A Major Scale   Fingering Type 4

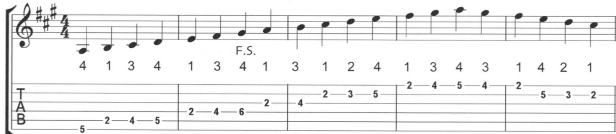

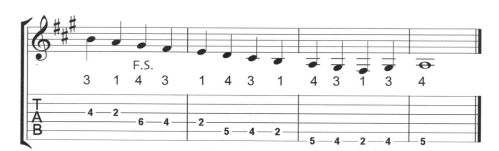

A hot Country lick using pick and fingers. Make sure you don't let any of the notes ring into each other. The last measure has a double bend lick that works well in Blues tunes as well. See ex. 126 below for another version of that lick.

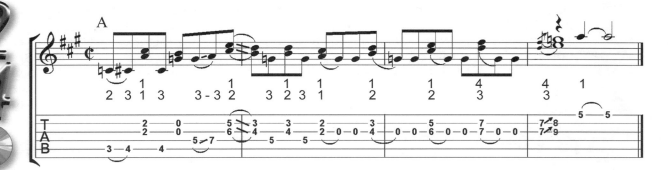

The concept of moveable shapes works great in Rock as well as Jazz. The first six notes are moved up and down in half steps. It creates a "slightly out" kind of sound which can add new life to tired old licks. Be careful with all the pull-offs, they're there as much for phrasing as they are to make the picking easier. If you tried to pick every single note, it would be much harder!

Double bends can sound a bit like an organ lick often used in the Blues. It will fit into Blues, Rock, Country, Rockabilly and more. Keep your 3rd and 4th finger glued together as you bend, it will help the pitches stay in tune. Use pick and finger for this one, you'll have a stronger attack that way.

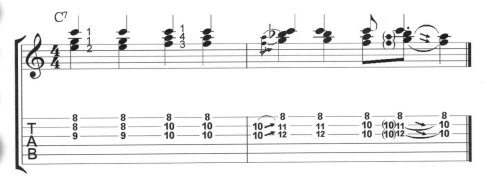

BASS SNAPPIN' & SLAPPIN':

I've always envied the bass player's ability to slap and pop those funky bass lines. Bassist extraordinaire and recording session giant Abraham Laboriel and I went through Berklee together and his incredibly funky style of playing inspired me to develop my own way of trying to get that sound on the guitar. Use fingers only for this example. Your thumb snaps the strings from *below* and moves upwards. Your first finger yanks the string up and snaps it. The more "vicious" you are, the better this will sound. The hardest part is the fretting hand slap, indicated by the large **X** in the center of the staff. Keep your fingers flat as they hit the strings to get a clear percussive sound. This will make more sense after you watch me play it in my video segment. See ex. 295 and 332 for more.

THE DIFFERENCE TONE:

Sometimes called a *combination tone*, *sum tone* or a *difference tone* , this is a phenomena that happens when two notes are played simultaneously while using distortion. When these intervals are played, you will hear a third tone whose frequency is the sum or difference of the two frequencies. The discovery of this phenomena is credited to the violinist Giuseppe Tartini and so the tones are also called Tartini tones. Rather than getting into the complex formulas as to how or why this happens, I'll just show you some of the things I've discovered over the years.
Although the difference tone is always present, like the overtone series (see ex. 133), it's not always easy to hear. If you use a good distortion box and a decent amp, you'll hear them loud and clear.

THE POWER CHORD:

How did the power chord get it's name? I have no idea, but, I think it's because of the difference tone. I'm sure most of the rockers out there have never heard of a difference tone before so they certainly weren't thinking, "Man, this intermodulation distortion thing creating that low octave is really powerful...hey, let's call it a power chord!" Here's what happens. Play the note E on the fifth string and a B on the fourth, that's a perfect fifth interval, the difference tone created will be another E one octave below the E you're playing.

Try this example and listen for the extra bass part you get for free.

D.T. stands for difference tone.

The interval of a perfect fourth produces a difference tone two octaves below the high note. The difference tone should be very easy to hear in this example.

Play this example and listen for the root, fifth bass line that's created.

DIFFERENCE TONES continued.

So far, all of the difference tones have been one or two octaves below one of the notes played. However, when you play the interval of a major 6th, a third note is produced different from the two you're playing. In this example, the D power chord produces a low D as expected, but the sixth interval of D and B produces a low G which makes a complete G major triad.

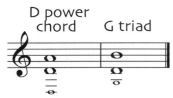

This one is my favorite example of a difference tone. Play the fourth interval (F# and B) and you get a difference tone of a B two octaves below. Now, bend the F# up to G# while letting the high B ring, you'll hear the low B difference tone slide all the way down to a low E. Not very useful on a gig, but fun.

When you're cutting your first CD and about to make it as a rock star, use this lick on the end of a tune in E, after you've sold a million albums, kids all over the world will be trying to figure out how you got one note to bend up and the other to go down. ☺

THE 4 STRING DIXIELAND BANJO EFFECT:

Take a piece of paper and fold it into the shape below, 3 or 4 folds are plenty. Long enough to weave, over/under, into the strings. Slide it back to the bridge. This will produce a muffled sound with a bit of a buzz to it. No one will ever mistake you for a tenor Banjo player, but it will sound a lot closer than it would without it. Use this effect on ex. 242.

Similar to ex. 114, but using different notes, this lick will work at the end of the 12 bar Blues progression when you want to musically tell the band, "I'm not done yet, I'm going to play another 12 bars."

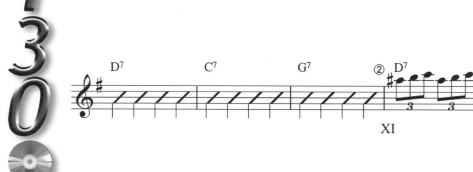

This is a continuation of the "Memphis Vamp" you saw back in ex. 75. I've added a bunch of variations going from simple to complex. The "commas" (for the first example only) mean to release the chord to make it shorter. The use of triplets really makes this rhythm come alive. It's fairly hard to get them to sound just right, but if you use the triplet picking example at the bottom as your guide, you'll have greater success. The G# chord is slid into the A chord and immediately released creating a ghost note, a note that's inferred rather than heard, it's indicated by putting the chord in parenthesis.

These 3 voicings are to be used for the example. Whenever you see an A chord, play the first chord, a D, play the second and an A[7], play the third.

Use this picking pattern for the triplets.
Down-up-down, down-up-down.

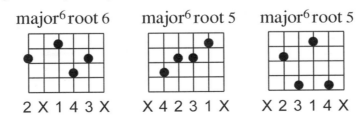

A major 6th chord is built from the root, 3rd, 5th and 6th degrees of a major scale. Major 6th chords are a staple of Western Swing as well as Jazz. Here are 3 of the most common ways to play them. Remember, you can *always* substitute a major 6th chord for a plain major chord or a major 7th chord. Of course you must be aware of the style you're playing. Putting a major 6th chord in a Rock tune could sound pretty weak.

THE OVERTONE SERIES:

Everytime you pick a string, many different notes sound at the same time. You may not hear them all but they're there. They are what's known as the overtone series. As the diagram below shows, each time a string is cut into halves, quarters, thirds, fourths, etc. different harmonics occur. We're all accustomed to hearing the natural harmonics that occur on the 12th, 7th and 5th frets, but, have you tried to find the other places harmonics occur?

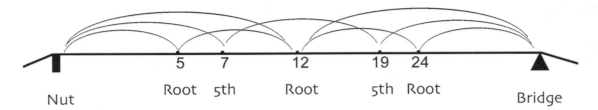

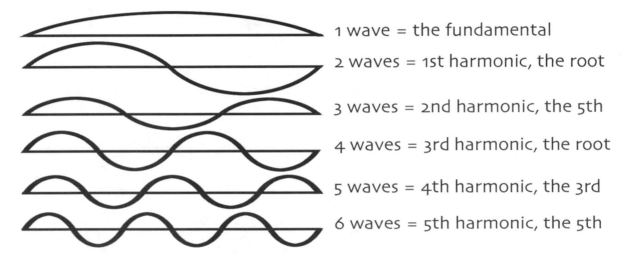

1 wave = the fundamental

2 waves = 1st harmonic, the root

3 waves = 2nd harmonic, the 5th

4 waves = 3rd harmonic, the root

5 waves = 4th harmonic, the 3rd

6 waves = 5th harmonic, the 5th

The overtone series from the fundamental of C.

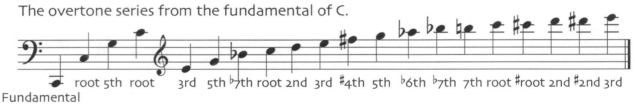

This graphic shows where all the overtones fall on the low E string. The higher in the series you go, heading towards the nut, the closer together they get and the harder they are to hear. Using distortion helps them sound more clearly and that's one reason why Rock players use so many pinch harmonics (ex.166). Once you pass the 12th fret, they repeat in reverse order getting closer together as you approach the bridge. This is good to know when you looking for specific harmonics using the pinch or other fingered harmonic techniques.

This example uses the harmonics that are fairly easy to play. The "#" before a number in the tab section means the note is a little in front of the fret, a "♭" for behind the fret.

A fun example with all natural harmonics. The next time you're playing a song in G or Em, throw this in at the end and everyone will think you're "Mr. Guitar!"

Here is the classic Bossa Nova rhythm. The thumb stays steady on the half note alternating bass pattern, while the chords (played with fingers 1, 2 and 3) play the syncopated rhythm above. It will take a while to get comfortable with this polyrhythm. You'll find yourself anticipating the "and" of 4 with the bass note when you should be waiting for beat one in the next measure. Tap your foot "in two" along with the bass. Anytime a piece of music is in cut time, you should tap your foot on beats 1 and 3.

I heard this years ago in a tune called *Papa Was a Rollin' Stone*. It always stayed with me because it sounded so smooth and sexy. Just pick the first unison bend and then slide and bend to the other pitches. Repeat the procedure in measure 2. Be careful to stay in tune, these are *unison* bends after all.

The Jazz example below is a C minor pentatonic scale taken from the key of E♭. It could also be called an E♭ major pentatonic scale. Here it's functioning as minor because of the chord it's being used over. In a way, that's the secret of all the modes. It's not so much the notes that are being played, it's how they sound against the chord that's being played at that moment. What makes this example stand out is the shape of it. It uses fourth intervals instead of the typical thirds. It has a much more interesting quality that way.

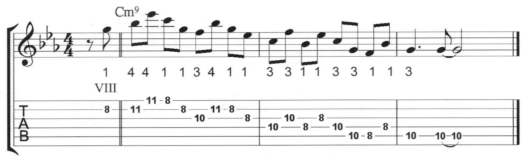

THE CLARINET SOUND:

Clarinet! Who wants to sound like a Clarinet? Well, you're right, but, the point of this example is to give you another color to add to your palette. We all pick the strings in about the same area of the guitar. Usually between the front and rear pickup. That's all well and good, but I discovered one day, that if you pick 12 frets above the fingered notes, the sound quality changes dramatically. It takes on a wooden or hollow sound vaguely similar to that of a Clarinet.
On the recording you'll hear me play this by picking in the regular area first, then picking approximately 12 frets above each note. You don't have to be exactly 12 frets above, but close does count.
You won't be putting any Clarinet players out of work, not that there's any work for them anyway, but you will have another sweet sound at you disposal for when the mood hits you.

AVAILABLE TENSIONS:

An Em^7 chord shows up in the key of C and you want to play your favorite min^9 voicing, wrong! The note for tension 9 on the Em chord (F♯) is not available in the key of C so you can't use it. That's what available tensions are all about. Not just for chord scales but just as importantly for what tensions you can use on your rhythm chord forms.
Here's the list:
If it's a I chord, you can add 6, 7 and 9. A IV chord, 6, 7, 9 and ♯11. A IIm^7 or VIm^7, 9 and 11. A $IIIm^7$, 11. A $VIIm^{7♭5}$, 11. A II^7 or V^7, 9 and 13. A III^7, VI^7 or VII^7, ♭9 and ♭13. A IV^7, 9, ♯11 and 13. All nondiatonic min^7 chords, 9 and 11. All nondiatonic major chords with diatonic roots, 6, 7, and 9. All nondiatonic major chords with nondiatonic roots, 6, 7, 9 and ♯11. Too many times the chord chart will just tell you that the chord is major, minor or dominant and you have to know what tensions you can or can not add.

ECHO • ECHO • ECHO • ECHO • ECHO

You get the idea. Echo has been around since prehistoric man first yelled inside a cave and heard his voice reflect off the walls and come back to him as an echo. It must have scared the heck out of him! Way back in our own electronic prehistoric period, the 1950's, tape echo was discovered. A tape recorder has 2 heads, a record head and a playback head. By listening to the record head *and* the playback head at the same time an echo is produced. Then they figured out how to move the playback head further away from the record head to get echoes of different lengths. The famous "Echoplex" had 4 different playback heads that were movable to create different delay times. Then in the 60's and 70's analog delay was created. It was much simpler to use but was pretty noisy. The late 70's saw the first digital delays and the rest is history. Now every stomp box and rack unit has some kind of digital delay built into it. Les Paul and Chet Atkins made the effect popular as a gimmick and then everyone started using it. It's a great way to enhance the sound of the guitar and a fun way to create some really neat licks.

If you set the repeat to happen one quarter beat after the original note, you will hear diatonic thirds when you play an eighth note scale. If you have 3 or 4 repeats, the thirds become triads and four part chords.

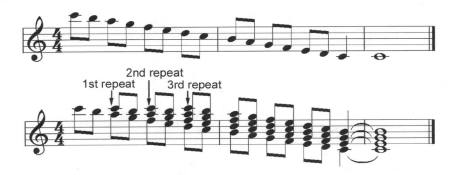

Try it with a whole tone scale and get a kind of spooky sounding lick.

Most of the time, when you hear an echo, you perceive it to be occurring either a quarter or eighth beat later than the original attack.

But, if you set it to occur on the 4th sixteenth of the beat and then play staccato eighth note licks, you can sound like a real speed demon. The beauty of this lick is that it doesn't sound like an echo lick and you only have to play half as fast as it sounds!

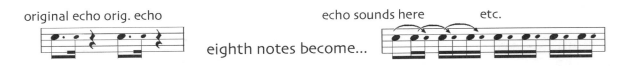

eighth notes become...

DIGITAL DELAY DEXTERITY:

If you've spent a little time with the previous page and understand how to use this echo hot lick technique, this example will amaze all your metal friends. I used licks like this in a concert at Berklee and had to have the drummer play to a click track. If his time wandered even a little bit, I'd be in big trouble. The tune was really fast! I started it with my back to the audience so they'd think I was actually playing as fast as it sounded. Even after I turned around, people told me later, "Man, you were playing so fast, it didn't even look like your hand was moving!" ...Heh, heh.

The most important thing to remember is to make all the notes very short. If you don't, they will bleed into each other and ruin the effect. If you really were playing this fast, each note would be very short anyway. Think of it this way, you have to leave room between each note you play for the echoed notes.

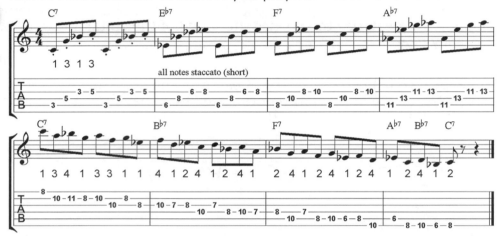

Here's what it sounds like. Play it fast enough and you'll amaze your next audience. It takes a while to get comfortable with this technique, but it's so hot, it's worth the effort.

1
4
4

THE THEREMIN:

The Theremin was invented in 1919 by a Russian physicist named Lev Termen (later changed to Leon Theremin). Not only does it look like no other instrument, it is the only instrument that is played without being touched. Two antennas protrude from the Theremin, one controlling pitch, and the other controlling volume. As your hand approaches the vertical antenna, the pitch gets higher, approaching the horizontal antenna makes the volume softer. Because there is no physical contact with the instrument, playing the Theremin requires precise skill and an excellent sense of pitch. One rather fuzzy night on a gig in Thule, Greenland (near the Polar ice cap) when I was 19, the band was in the middle of what we called a "Freak Out" back then. What that means is we all played whatever we wanted to play with little concern for what anybody else was playing. I grabbed a drum stick and started running it up and down the strings while using a lot of distortion. It sounded pretty good. The next day, when my head cleared, I tried it again and realized I could actually play melodies with this technique. It reminded me of the Theremin sound I had heard in those low budget sci-fi movies from the 50's. The Theremin has been used live or in the studio by a diverse group of artists including The Beach Boys, Led Zeppelin, Incubus, Aerosmith, Motley Crue and Phish.

You have to be careful with your intonation when doing this because the pitch comes from where you touch the strings, not from the frets themselves. Use as much distortion as you can get. The drum stick should *not* be new. It helps if it's been pretty well beaten up. Keep the strings quiet, holding them dead around the 3rd fret with your fretting hand, and use the drumstick like a slide. Hold the drum stick like a pencil (see photo) and use as much vibrato as needed for the style you're playing.

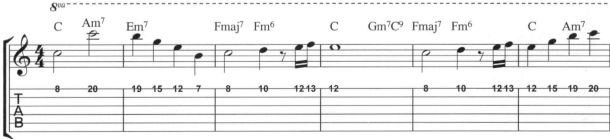

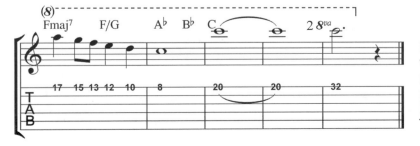

I got a little carried away with the orchestration on the recording. I was picturing myself performing with the Boston Symphony with my Tele and a drum stick!

BASIC THEORY - DIATONIC CHORDS and MODES:

If you start with a C major scale and stack up 3 more notes on top of each scale note a third away from the previous one, you end up with the 7 diatonic (built from the scale) chords in a major key. The easy thing to remember when building chords is that if the scale note is on a line, so are the other three notes, if it's in a space, so are the others.

The resulting pattern of chord types is major[7], min[7], min[7], major[7], dom[7], min[7] and min[7(b5)]. This pattern stays the same in all major keys, just change the names of the scale notes to suit the new key. To help us identify these chords, we assign roman numerals to them. The I chord, the II chord, etc. The Nashville Number System, which is similar, is described in ex. 330. So, if someone says, "Let's jam on a 1, 6, 2, 5 in the key of G," you'll know it will be Gmaj[7] (I), Em[7] (VI), Am[7] (II), and D[7] (V) because the type of chord doesn't change, just the root name to suit the key you're in. Each diatonic chord has a corresponding modal name. These are listed below.

C Major Scale

The 7 Diatonic Chords in the Key of C

Imaj[7]..........Cmaj[7]......Ionian mode
IIm[7]..........Dm[7]........Dorian mode
IIIm[7].........Em[7]........Phrygian mode
IVmaj[7]......Fmaj[7]......Lydian mode
V[7].............G[7]..........Mixolydian mode
VIm[7].........Am[7]........Aeolian mode
VIIm[7b5].....Bm[7(b5)]....Locrian mode

MODAL CHARACTERISTICS:

Each mode has something unique about it that makes it sound different from the others. Here is the formula for building each mode when starting with a major scale. In other words, D major has an F♯ and C♯ in it. To make D major into D Dorian, you must flat the 3rd and the 7th degrees.

Ionian...............Normal major scale
Dorian..............♭3 and ♭7
Phrygian..........♭2, ♭3, ♭6 and ♭7
Lydian..............♯4
Mixolydian.......♭7
Aeolian............♭3, ♭6 and ♭7
Locrian.............♭2, ♭3, ♭5, ♭6 and ♭7

MORE MODES:

Here are the 7 diatonic modes starting on their root. Of course, in the real world, you start wherever you happen to be at the time. It sounds really lame to start on the root of a mode each time a new chord appears. As you can see, all of this mode stuff turns out to be nothing more than a major scale from different degrees. So what's the big deal about modes? I don't know! I think people make them out to be more complicated and scarier then they need to be. The only thing that really matters are the chord tones of each chord. When you fill in the gaps between chord tones with notes from the key, surprise, you get a mode.

If you're on an Fmaj⁷ chord, in the key of C, playing the chord tones of F, A, C and E and you want to play a scale lick to get you someplace else, you take the notes from the key you're in at the moment and fill in the gaps. That means add a G, B natural and D between your chord tones and the result will be the correct scale. In this case, it would be F Lydian, otherwise known as C major or C Ionian.

The notes in ( ) parentheses are "avoid notes" or "passing tones." That means they're used for passing from one note to another but not for landing on or sustaining. Avoid notes are always a half step above a chord tone.

Here's a little example of how you might practice running modes on a chord progression. Remember, it's still all a C major scale no matter what mode you're using. Even though I started on the root each time, you should try to weave these modes together from whichever note you're on at the moment.

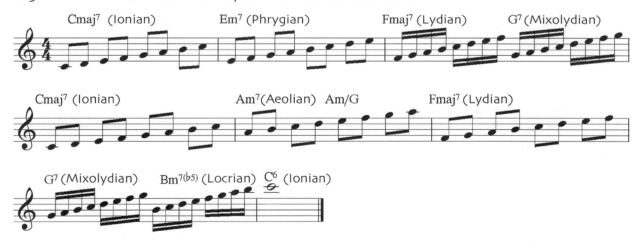

GUIDE TONES:

The 3rd and 7th of a chord are called the guide tones. They tell you if the chord is major or minor and maj⁷ or dom⁷. They are the *good notes* that you should always strive to play each time a new chord occurs. You can call them "target notes" as well. Very often they resolve from the 3rd to the 7th and the 7th to the 3rd as the next chord appears. When learning how to play on changes, one thing you must get good at is being able to play the guide tones of each chord. When running modes, try to make a guide tone from one chord connect to a guide tone of the next chord. Analyze some of the Jazz licks in this book and you'll see how this all works.

CHORD SCALES THE EASY WAY:

Chord Scales are just modes and modes are just parts of a scale. Here is the easiest way I know to make sure you'll always play the correct scales in a tune. As my dear friend and former Chairman of the Guitar Department at Berklee, Bill Leavitt, once said, "The ears don't have eyes." What that means is simple. When you're hearing chords go by, you are hearing a particular key center. Every time a chord shows up that isn't in that key, your ears have to adjust to the chord tones in that new chord. Your "ears" can't "see" what chord is coming next in a tune, so it shouldn't affect how you play on the chord of the moment.

In chord progression analysis, you might say that the E^7 chord below is a V^7 of the VIm. That's true, but we don't care where the E^7 is going, we only care how it affects the key of C we've been hearing. To say it another way, "Try to stay in one key all the time." If a chord shows up with a new note in it, like the $G^\sharp$ in the E^7 chord, add the $G^\sharp$ to your C scale and don't think about it again. The resulting scale will be correct, even if you have no idea what it is. It doesn't matter if you can name the scale, it only matters that you play some $G^\sharp$s in your C scale over the E^7 chord. Just so you'll know, I've put the "actual" name of the scale under each chord. Even on a chord as unusual as the $D^{\flat 9}$ at the end of the example, if you spell the chord to include tension 13 you get $D^\flat$, F, $A^\flat$, $C^\flat$, $E^\flat$ and $B^\flat$. If you add those notes to your C scale, you'll end up playing an $A^\flat$ melodic minor scale ($D^\flat$ Lydian $^\flat 7$ mode) whether you know it or not! Chord tones are the secret to all improvisation, not modes. You *must* learn how to spell and play the chord tones of every type of chord there is. You need to be able to "see" all the thirds and sevenths in each chord as they go by so you can choose which ones to play.

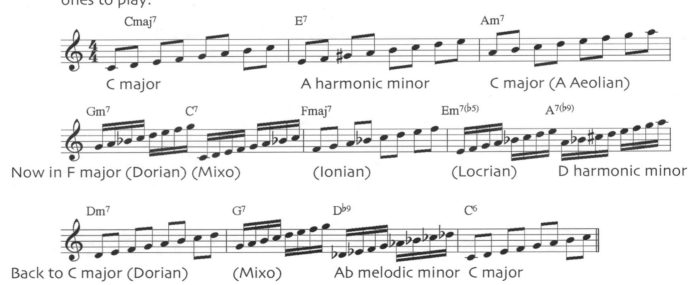

C major   A harmonic minor   C major (A Aeolian)

Now in F major (Dorian) (Mixo)   (Ionian)   (Locrian)   D harmonic minor

Back to C major (Dorian)   (Mixo)   Ab melodic minor   C major

SPELLING CHORDS MADE EASY:

If you know your key signatures (see ex. 80, bottom of the page), you can spell any chord in no time at all. Here's how: Let's say you had to spell $E^{\flat 9}$. First, you know that all dom^7 chords are V chords, so in what key is $E^\flat$ the V chord? The answer is $A^\flat$. Next, think of the key signature of $A^\flat$, there are 4 flats ($B^\flat$, $E^\flat$, $A^\flat$, $D^\flat$). In your mind, picture the music staff, place the note $E^\flat$ on the first line, stack up 4 more notes (G, B, D, F) look at the key signature and see which notes are affected. You'll end up with $E^\flat$, G, $B^\flat$, $D^\flat$, and F. You're done, that's how to spell $E^{\flat 9}$. Easy, right? Just remember, if the root is in a space, the next 3 or 4 notes are in spaces, if the root is on a line, the next 3 or 4 notes are on lines. You'll have the correct letter names very quickly, then all that's left to do is to add the flats or sharps from the key signature.

149

Another Jazz example that proves the point about parallel licks. You start with the first measure's chromatic little thing and just walk the whole pattern up the neck "hoping" that the notes fit the chords as they go by.

If we analyze them, we find that it's $\flat 7$ on the Dm, $\flat 5$ on the G7, root on the Dm, $\sharp 5$ on the G7, root on the Em, $\flat 13$ on the A7, 9 on the Em, $\flat 7$ on the A7, $\sharp 11$ and 5 on the D7 and 13 and $\flat 7$ on the D$\flat$. Amazing! They all work out to be notes that are, more or less, available tensions on those chords (see ex. 141 for more on available tensions). Sometimes you just get lucky.

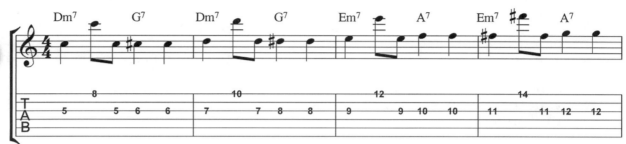

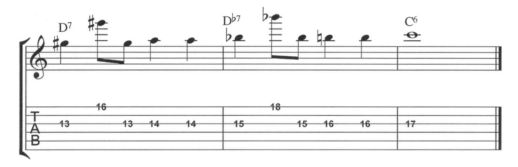

150

Here is a typical Latin rhythm guitar pattern. You can use it in a lot of 50's and 60's tunes, in a cha cha, in Italian and Greek songs and anywhere else a Latin type dance rhythm is needed. The wavy line pointing up means to strum deliberately using a down stroke so you can hear all the strings, like a very short drum roll. The first string will sound "on" the beat so you must start the downstroke before the beat. Try using an upstroke now and then just to change it around a little. The word "simile" means, continue to play in a similar manner. It's the easy way out of writing those voicings over and over again.

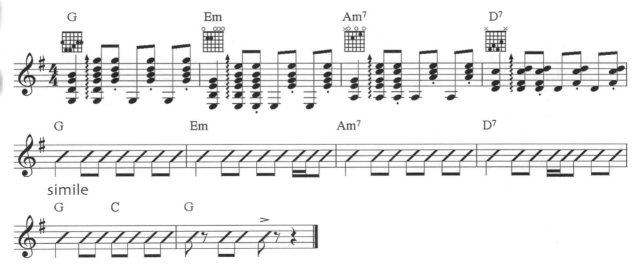

CROSSING THE BAR LINE:

No, I don't mean cutting to the front of the line to get into some cool, hip nightclub! I'm talking about the importance of what you play across the bar line or when the chord changes.

I've mentioned *guide tones* in ex. 147. They're the "good notes" that you use to connect one of the guide tones from one chord to one of the guide tones of another chord. The biggest mistake most players make when they're learning to play on changes (in any style) is to stop everytime a new chord shows up. They're thinking too much about what to play next and the result sounds more like stuttering than music. You'll sound better if you just play a few notes in a measure, rather than trying to impress eveybody with how fast you are, and resolve the last note of that measure to a strong note in the next measure.

The general public (your audience) doesn't care what you play inside a given measure but they do notice if you don't connect your ideas across the bar line or when the chord changes. If a measure of Dm⁷ is followed by one of G⁷, you can whip out all your cool Dorian and Mixolydian licks but if you don't play a C resolving to a B over the barline as the chords change, it won't sound smooth.

Now I know some people will argue with the way I approach this idea, but I'm telling you what will sound good *the first time you try it*.

As with a lot of the rules in this book, there are probably as many exceptions. Let's let the pros deal with the exceptions and we'll just stick with the rules that work all the time and help you sound like a decent player while you're still struggling to get it all together.

This is a Country Ragtime style example and I use the chromatic scale to create movement. It really leads the listener and keeps their interest as it moves higher and higher. Work on playing this with a smooth and equal pick attack and as always, start slow and gradually work up the tempo. The faster the better.

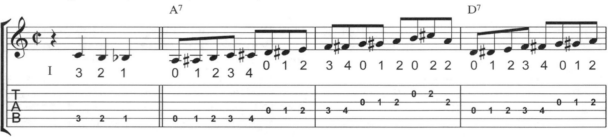

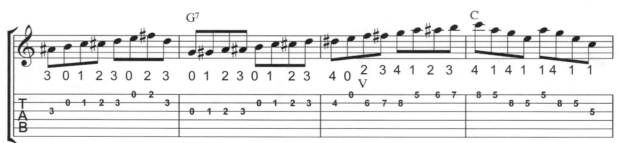

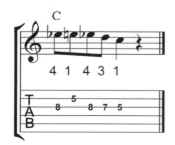

The first part is a typical Jazz II-V lick. The second part uses chromatic approaches to each of the chord tones on the E♭maj⁷ chord.

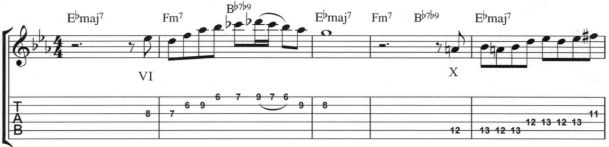

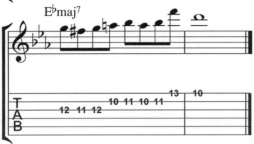

Any major chord can have tension 6, 7, and 9 added to it to make it fuller and hipper sounding. It all depends on the style you're playing at the time. If the major chord is a IV or any major chord with a nondiatonic root, you can also add ♯11 to it. Quite often, the ♯11 is added to the very last chord of a song. It doesn't belong there, but it sounds so good, we've become accustomed to hearing it there. Major chords either function as a I chord or a IV chord, so you only have 2 choices of scales to play against them, Ionian or Lydian. If the chord is a major chord with a scale tone root (Cmaj⁷, Emaj⁷, Bmaj⁷ etc.) play Ionian. If its root is nondiatonic, (E♭maj⁷, A♭maj⁷ etc.) play Lydian.

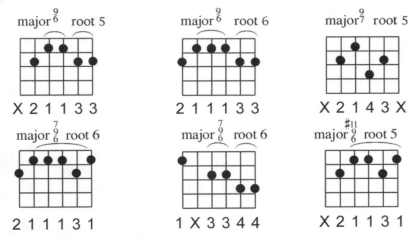

A min⁷♭5 chord is built from the root, flat 3rd, flat 5th and flat 7th of a major scale. Here are 3 good ways to play them. A typical progression that uses a IIm⁷⁽♭5⁾ usually goes to a V⁷⁽♭9⁾. The last voicing will give you a nice chromatic bass motion from its flat fifth down to the V chord's root. Min⁷⁽♭5⁾ almost always takes the Locrian mode. Sometimes, you can use a melodic minor scale from the chord's flat 3rd degree.

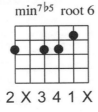

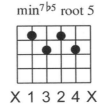

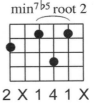

SITAR LICKS:

Here is a passage that has phrasing similar to what a sitar player might play (see ex. 326 for more on the Sitar). The lick is "displaced" which means the same rhythm is mathematically moved to the right so that it begins on a different beat each time. In this case, it starts on beat one, then the "and" of 2, then 4, then the "and" of 1, then beat 3 before resolving in the third measure. Try bending the notes instead of using slurs, it will sound more authentic. On the recording I play it as written the first time and with bends the second time. Because of the way the Sitar is built, they will often bend a whole phrase from one starting note. They might play a G then bend it to A and then further to B♭, C or higher.

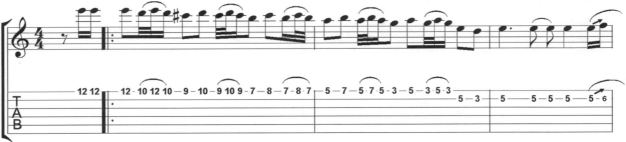

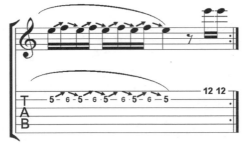

A fairly accurate sitar sound can be made by shaving a 1/4 inch flat side into a regular steel guitar bar. This new flat side will buzz just enough to give you a nice sitar sound. Lay it on the strings and move it around like a lap steel or dobro player would. It helps if your action is higher than normal.

Check out this cool trick. Get some small corks from your local hardware store, put one between the 1st and 2nd string, one between the 3rd and 4th string and one between the 5th and 6th string as shown in the photo. Make sure they float above the pickups or pick guard. It won't work if the bottom of the cork touches anything. To play them, you can hit the top of the corks with your finger, a mallet, a pencil, whatever. You can also just hit the strings wherever you want. Try different pickup combinations for different timbres.
To me, this effect sounds a little like tympani or some kind of metal drum. It would make a great rhythm track for a loop or to add some other-world quality to your recording. It just goes to show you, experiment! Look around the house and see what else you can find to make some new sounds.

PICKING HAND RHYTHM GUITAR STROKE:

In my opinion, the best way to stroke the strings for rhythm guitar playing is with a motion I call the "wrist twist." There are a few ways to think of this motion.

First, hold your arm out straight, imagine you had a house key in your hand. Put that key into a door lock and turn it clockwise to open the lock. That wrist twisting motion is what you want for ease of playing, control and power. If your doing it correctly, you should notice that your hand seems to be pivoting under the first knuckle of your first finger.

Second, imagine you wanted to flick a piece of dust off your shirt around the area of your belly (with a closed hand). By twisting your wrist instead of using your whole forearm, you not only increase the control you have over the pick but you use much less space to complete the stroke.

Picking from the elbow, which many players do, is OK for some situations, but for fast, complex rhythms, you'll get tired much to quickly picking that way. The same holds true for single note playing, the smaller the distance your pick has to cover, the faster you can cover that distance.

1.

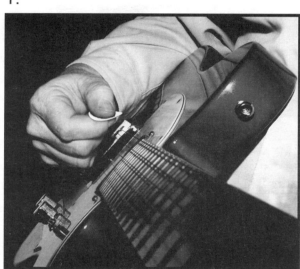

2.

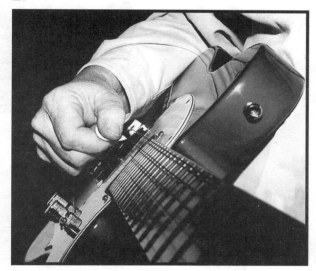

3.

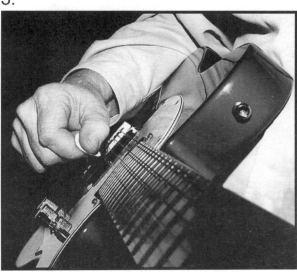

4.

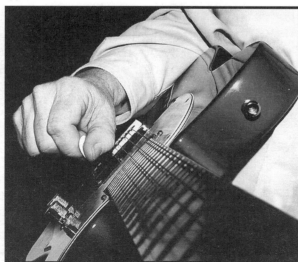

ARTIFICIAL or FINGERED HARMONICS:

You've seen how all the natural harmonics happen and there are a lot of pitches to choose from, but what if you want notes that don't occur naturally? You use fingered harmonics. As the photo shows, put the pick between your thumb and middle finger and reach out with the first finger. The first finger touches lightly 12 frets above (or 5 or 7 frets) the fretted note and you pick behind the finger to create the harmonic. This technique will allow you to play arpeggios, melodies, background lines and more. In this Country example, the fretting hand never moves, but where you chime the harmonics does. Remember, the tab tells you where to touch, not where to finger.

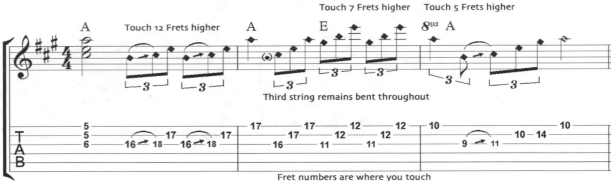

Third string remains bent throughout

Fret numbers are where you touch

A nice technique with artificial harmonics is to just harmonic one of the two notes you're playing. In the first 2 measures, harmonic the low note of the 6ths. This turns them into 3rds, or, if you play 3rds in the same way, they become 6ths. The second part of the example is a descending scale run where the high note is actually the low note played as a harmonic. Use your ring finger for the non-harmonic notes. Keep everything ringing.

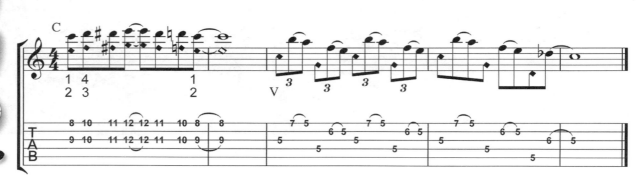

161

Here's a Folk fingerpicking example using the thumb-one-thumb-two pattern shown in ex. 88. This versatile pattern will work for any Folk or Pop ballad. The example below is in the Folk style. It can easily be adapted to sound like a Travis style Ragtime rhythm. See ex. 199 for more. Remember to make the hammer-ons and pull-offs sound good and clear.

162

This Jazz/Rock Fusion example is played over a dom7 chord because you can play a lot of altered tensions and they'll still sound OK. Constant structures are a popular thematic motif. In this example, there are a series of major triad arpeggios moving down in whole steps against an E7 chord. By themselves they would sound pretty strange, but strung together in a constant pattern of whole steps they work. The most important thing to remember with licks like this is to start on a strong note and end on a strong note. What you play between them isn't as important as the first and last note.

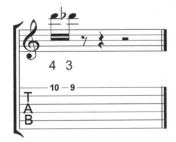

THE BANJO:

Originally invented in Africa, the banjo has evolved into two main types. The 4 string banjo, also called the Plectrum (low to high D, B, G, C) or Tenor banjo (A, D, G, C) which is the older of the two and usually heard in Dixieland music, and the 5 string banjo (Ghigh, D, G, B, D) commonly called a Bluegrass banjo. They even have a 6 string version for those of us who don't have the time to learn to play it in the proper tuning. There are many ways to play it, but most consist of either fast strumming or complex finger picking.

In the 19th century the banjo was found primarily in African American traditional music and minstrel shows. Although the banjo is usually found in Country and Bluegrass music, it has been a large part of other ethnic cultures as well.

4 string tenor banjo

Basically the banjo is a drum with strings on it. Originally a calf or goat skin was stretched over a wood rim but today it's usually made from polyester.

Some of the great old timers were Burl Ives, Grandpa Jones, Uncle Dave Macon and the father of Bluegrass banjo, Earl Scruggs. Current players such as Bela Fleck, Alison Brown and Tony Trischka are taking their music out of the traditional Bluegrass world and into Jazz and other realms often just called "new acoustic music."

5 string Bluegrass banjo

(Thanks to Deering Banjos for the photographs. Visit www.DeeringBanjos.com)

Warm up exercises are important to your musical health. Like runners or other athletes, you should warm up your muscles before any strenuous playing or practicing. This exercise is a simple 4-notes-per-string pattern. It will help you increase the coordination between your picking hand and your fretting hand. Start with eighth notes at a quarter beat equal to 60 bpm on your metronome. Keep a diary of your progress. Increase the bpm each day, a little at a time. Never go to a higher number until you can play an exercise perfectly at a given setting. For variations on this exercise, move your first finger a fret below your other 3 fingers. For the widest stretch, move your first finger a fret below and your fourth finger a fret above. If at any time, something hurts...*stop!* It shouldn't hurt. You may be overdoing it and need to rest.

165

This photo shows the proper hand position for string bending. You will have more power and more control with your thumb up around the neck (no matter what your guitar teacher said!).

Also, you should almost always bend with at least 2 fingers on the same string. This will give you much more control over the bend. At times, you may hear other strings making noise as you release a bend, to stop this from happening, use your fretting hand's first finger as a mute for the top 4 strings. Just lay it across them when you're not using it.

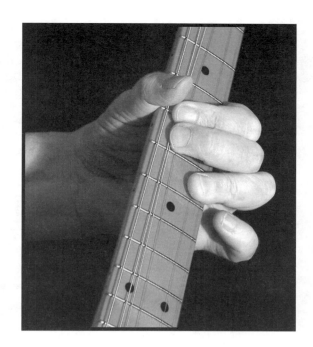

166

PINCH HARMONICS:

Usually played in Rock, Blues and Country, the pinch harmonic (sometimes called a whistler) is a very effective tool for adding a little extra expression to your solos. You wouldn't use it very often or for very long when you do use it. Like most unique sounds, overuse takes away their ability to peak the listeners interest. Forgetting what I just said, I used it for the whole example just so you can hear it. As a rule, you use it at the climax of a phrase or anytime you want a note to really stand out. To play this effect, bring the pick further into your hand so that just the smallest amount of pick is visible. As you pick the string, the string hits the pick and then hits the skin on the side of your thumb. This contact creates the harmonic.

Usually, you don't care what pitch is created when using the pinch harmonic, *but,* if you aim for 12 frets (or 7 or 5) above your fretting hand, you'll hear the lick an octave, an octave and a fifth or 2 octaves higher.

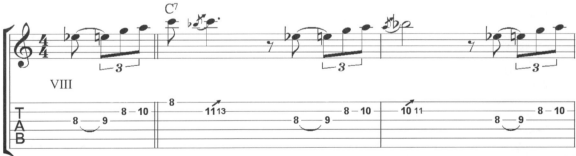

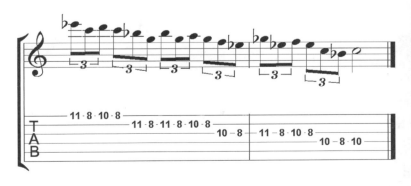

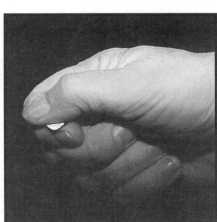

Using the interval of a perfect 4th is a good sound in R & B, Funk and Soul. In this example I overuse it, but that's just to give you some ideas. You've heard little bits of it used on Motown records as well as some of Hendrix's tunes. It has such a non-chordal sound that it fits almost anywhere. Using the major pentatonic scale as your melody note, just add a note a 4th below it and wander around the neck. It'll work just fine.

167

PERCUSSION TRICKS:

Claves are a pair of cylindrical hardwood sticks that are hit together to create percussive rhythms. They are used mostly in Latin music and particularly in the Bossa Nova. Here are some typical rhythms. You can "tune" the Claves to the key of the song by moving your fretting hand around until it's covering a fret that suits the key you're in.

168

168a   THE CLAVE

Hold the strings dead around the 17th fret

168b   THE GUIROS

The Guiros is a longnecked gord with ridges cut into it. A stick is scraped along its length creating a distinctive and recognizable sound. Add it into any Latin style song.

Scrape the edge of the pick on the 6th sting an inch in front of the bridge. Make the scrape towards the bridge last for a beat and a half, then a short scrape the other way. See ex. 74 and 86 for more.

CAREER OPTIONS IN THE MUSIC INDUSTRY

PERFORMANCE

Vocal/Instrumental Soloist
Music Conductor/Director
Group/Orchestra Member
Band Leader
Studio Musician
Church Musician
Product Demonstrator

COMPOSITION

Composer/Arranger for TV, Films,
Music Video, Animation, Claymation,
Show Music, Dramatic Music, Educa-
tional Material, Children's Music,
Operettas, Choral groups, Community
Theater
Arranger
Songwriter
Jingle Writer
Copyist/Editor
Orchestrator
Transcriber
Music Therapy

BUSINESS

Ad Sales Person
Music Book Publisher
Union Contractor
Song Publisher
Entertainment Lawyer
Independent Record Producer
Artist Promoter
Music Festival Coordinator
Music Publisher
Concert Hall Owner/Manager
Booking Agent
Musical Instrument Manufacturer
Recording Studio Owner
Film/TV Music Producer
Night Club Owner
Jingle Producer
Concert Promoter
Market Manager

Referral System Organizer
Accountant
Distributor
Broadcaster
Radio Consultant
Radio Program Director
Radio/TV Voice Over Artist
Rare Instrument Dealer/Appraiser
Retailer (CDs, Instruments etc.)
Manager (Band, Personal, Studio)
Inventor of Musical Novelties
Music Research and Development
Performance Rights Society (ASCAP,
BMI, SESAC)
International/Regional Marketing and
Development
A & R
Artist Relations
Business Affairs
Creative Services
Sales, Promotion, Marketing
Distribution
Legal Department
Operations
Publishing Affiliate

STYLES

Functions/General Business/Casuals
Country
Rock
Jazz
Blues
Metal
Punk
Pop
Funk
Reggae
Christian
Folk/Ethnic
Gospel
Latin
World
R & B
Soul
Rap

ENGINEERING AND OTHER TECHNICAL OCCUPATIONS

Tape, CD, DVD Manufacturer
Duplication Services
Mastering Lab Owner/Technician
Research and Design Specialist
Sound Company
Recording Engineer
Piano Tuner
Sound Engineer
Instrument Designer
Stage Technician
Acoustical Engineer
Music Software Inventor
Luthier
Instrument Repair Person
Inlay/Finish Specialist
Modification Technician
Computer Music Programmer
Programmer/Sound Creator and Sampling
Video Editing (Pre and Post Production)
Video/DVD Transfers

EDUCATION

Music School Administrator
Music Therapist
Music Librarian
Music Historian
Clinician
Ethnomusicologist
Teacher (Private Studio, Public Schools, College Professor, Independent/Secondary Schools)

RELATED ARTS

WRITING:
Lyricist
Librettist
Music Journalist
Author of Music Textbooks
Author of Pedigory Books
Music Journal Editor
Music Publications Staffer
Author of Musical Biographies

VISUAL ARTS:
Web Site Designer
Music Photographer
3D Animator
CD Cover design
Art Supplier
Logo Designer
Set Designer
Illustrator
Customized Labels
Choreographer

MISCELLANEOUS

Music Jewelry/Novelties
DJ/VJ
Inventor/Licensor
Wood/Parts Supplier
Instrument Insurance Agent
Digital Sales and Rentals
Gold Record Manufacturer
Limo Service
Printer
Specialty Merchandiser
Promotional Items (T-shirts, Souvenir Books)
Roadie

OTHER

Music Critic (Recorded and Live Performances)

TAPPED HARMONICS:

You've seen examples of fingered harmonics or artificial harmonics (ex. 159 and 160), well, here's yet another way to make them called tapped harmonics. I suggest you use the middle finger of your picking hand for this effect. Hit the string sharply and immediately bounce off to create the harmonic. As with all harmonics, you must be 12 frets above the fingered pitches. Bass players use this technique a lot because the thickness of their strings allows the harmonic to come out fairly easily. This technique has an extra bonus because you get the fundamental (original note) as well as the harmonic so it sounds like you're playing in octaves.

If tapping single note harmonics is fun, how about whole chords! Of course it helps if all of the notes in the chord are on one fret, but even if they cover two frets it will work almost as well. If they cover three frets or more you'll have to hit one section at a time. With an A¹³ on the 5th fret, strike the lower strings then strike the upper strings to get most of them to sound as harmonics. The sixteenth note triplets are little rolls played with the fingers indicated.

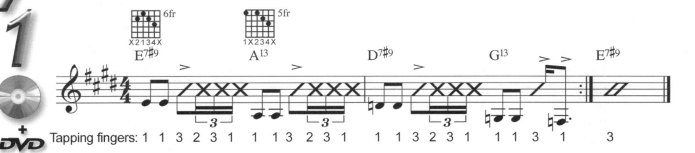

A good triplet based Blues lick with a few quarter step bends thrown in for color (the small arrows indicate the quarter step bends). No pull-offs, pick every note. This lick sounds best at a medium shuffle tempo.

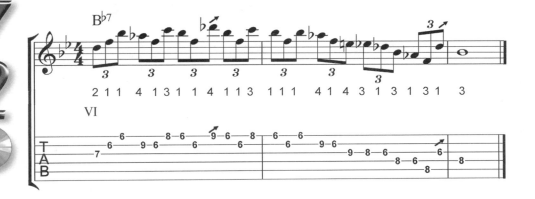

A single pull-off in a triplet can be moved around melodically to fit with the entire progression of this 16 bar Rock tune. It's fairly easy to get it going fast and it always sounds a lot harder than it is. That's a good thing. This example also doubles as a workout for your fingers. Play it nonstop a few times through and you'll feel your muscles tightening up.

BASIC BLUES or ROCK RHYTHM GUITAR:

Thousands of songs have been written over this groove. You've heard it played one way or another in Blues, Rock, Pop and Country tunes. This is probably one of the first rhythm parts a beginning guitarist will learn and it's always in the key of A because you can play all the chords in a Blues progression in the open position. Play this example with all down strokes when you use straight eighths and use alternate picking when you use swing eighths. Just because it's easy, don't think it's not a usable Blues lick. There are still plenty of songs that demand this rhythm. Transpose it to other keys without open strings. The basic pattern for the closed position version is shown at the bottom of the page.

On the recording, this example and ex. 175 are played back to back.

Closed position version.

175

Here is the same lick as the previous page but harmonized to create a more complex piano-like rhythm pattern. If you wanted to make a formula out of the way it's harmonized, it would be: play the I chord, then the IV chord over the I chord root, then the V minor chord (actually a I⁹ chord) over the I chord root. Keep banging away at the root while the top part is played more staccato or short. Use all down strokes to keep it driving unless you swing it and play a shuffle, then change to alternate picking.

On the recording, ex. 174 is played first, followed immediately by this one.

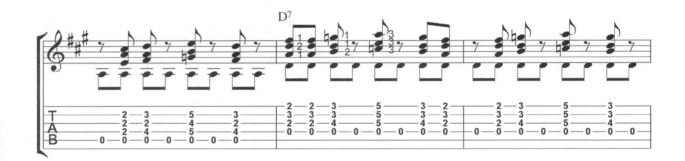

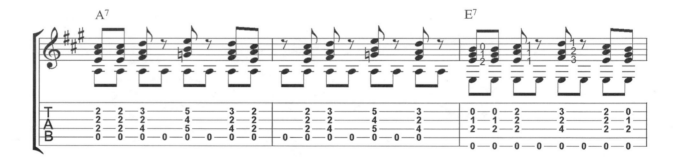

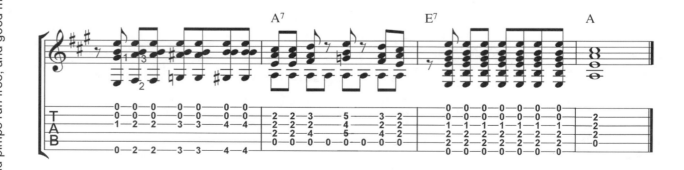

PICKING HAND TAPPING:

The flashy sound of tapping was brought into prominence by Van Halen in the 70's. The actual technique of using the picking hand to fret notes on the neck has been around since the dawn of amplification. A man named Jimmy White was playing standards with a two hand technique back in the 40's. Of course, since then, there's been innovators like Emmett Chapman and his Stick, Stanley Jordan and others. This example is the classic triplet triad argeggio lick made famous by Van Halen. I suggest that you use the middle finger of your picking hand to tap with. By using the middle finger, you won't have to change the position of your pick. Also, after the tap, bring your finger in towards your palm to re-pick the string. It's a more natural movement than flicking it away from the palm.

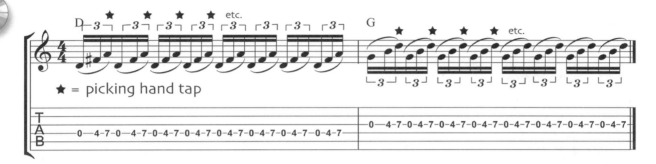

★ = picking hand tap

Here's a rhythmic variation on the triplet tapping lick using a double pull off before the usual triad lick. This pattern can be used to create a lot of other licks. Experiment!

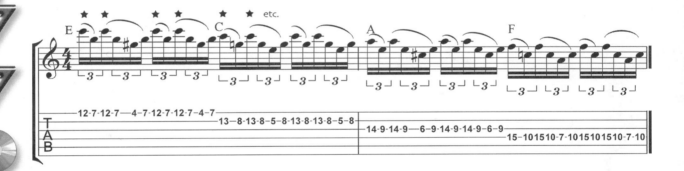

Trying to avoid the cliche sound of arpeggiating triads, I came up with this one using the Blues scale. It has the sound of a descending scale rather than an arpeggio. The pattern is: tap, pull-off, hammer-on the next lower string, then move the whole pattern over to the next group of strings.

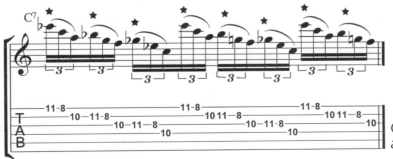

On the recording, ex. 176, 177 and 178 are played back to back.

A hot sounding Rock or Blues Lick that's not very hard to play fast because of all the pull-offs. Play it all in 8th position using the C Blues scale.

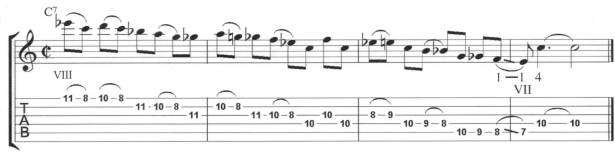

A nicely shaped Jazz lick that uses the C Phygian mode (A♭ major) against the C⁷ chord giving you a scale that has 1, ♭9, ♯9, 3, 4, 5, ♭6 and ♭7.

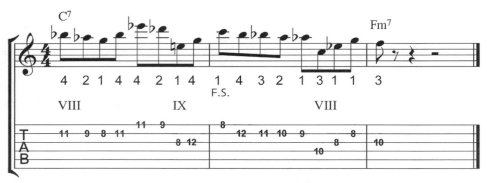

This fast Country/Bluegrass style lick moves all over the neck. Follow the position marks and fingerings carefully. The small x's are single dead notes created by lifting your fretting hand up just enough to make a dead click sound when picked.

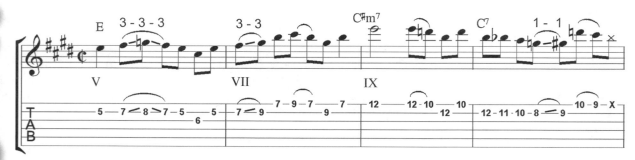

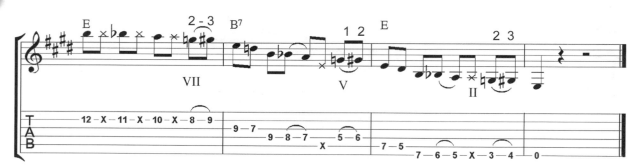

UPPER STRUCTURE TRIADS:

Pretty fancy sounding huh? The definition is: "Any 3 notes that create a major or minor triad and are extensions above the normal 1, 3, 5 and 7 of the host chord. Depending on the type of chord they're used on they could contain ♭5, ♯5, ♭9, 9, ♯9, 11, ♯11, ♭13 or 13, and occasionally some of the lower chord tones as well." Take a Cmaj⁷ chord, go to the note B and build up from there and see what you get. Above B would be D then since you can't use F (an avoid note) you could go to G. The result is B, D, and G or a G major triad. It contains the 7th, 9th and 5th of the Cmaj⁷ chord. So what do you do with this little gem of knowledge? You play G major triad arpeggios over your Cmaj⁷ chord and it sounds pretty hip! Here are some other choices of simple upper structure triads over a Cmaj⁷ chord.

Now, let's take it to the next level. If you force a Lydian sound onto the Cmaj⁷ chord (adding an F♯) you increase the amount of available upper structure triads. Now you can have D major, Bm, and Gmaj⁷ (not a triad but it sounds so good we'll use it anyway). When you're playing, try to randomly switch between C, D and G major triads as you work your way up or down the neck.

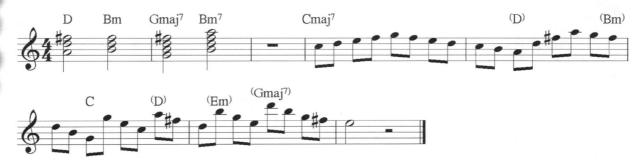

ROAD MAPS and other symbols you need to know about:
First Ending, play into the first ending then repeat to the beginning. Second Ending, play from the beginning, skip the first ending and play the second ending instead. D.S. al coda, go back to the sign 𝄋, use the second ending and play up to the Coda sign ⊕ then jump to the Coda. D.C. al coda, go back to the very beginning and play up to the Coda sign then jump to the Coda. You may see D.S or D.C al fine, play as before but stop at the fine (the end). Rit. (ritard) slow down. Fermata (⌒) hold longer than the the written value. Dynamic markings, *pp* (very soft), *p* (soft), *mp* (medium soft), *mf* (medium loud), *f* (loud), *ff* (very loud).

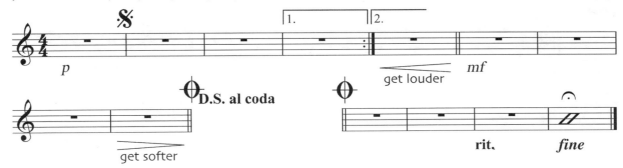

UPPER STRUCTURE TRIADS ON MINOR 7 CHORDS:

There's really only one that sounds hip and that's a maj7 arpeggio going up to tension 9. On Dm7, play an Fmaj7 arpeggio with 9 (F, A, C, E, G). If you look at it from Dm7, you have the 3rd, 5th, 7th, 9th and 11th. Of course there are others that sound good too, it's just that a maj7 arpeggio a minor third above a minor chord is one of my favorites. The following example uses C, Fmaj7 and Am triads against the Dm7 chord.

UPPER STRUCTURE TRIADS ON DOMINANT 7TH CHORDS:

Here's where it really gets interesting. You can imply so much more on a dominant chord than plain major or minor chords. The amount of upper structure triads are almost limitless. Here are a few of the simple ones you could use over a G7 chord: Bm♭5, Dm, Em and Fmaj. The Bm♭5 uses 3, 5 and ♭7, the Dm uses 5, ♭7 and 9th, the Em uses 13, root and 3, and the F uses ♭7, 9 and sus4. Once again, these are just a few of the possibilities. Try to figure out more on your own. What tensions would an Emaj and Amaj triad create over the G7 chord?

This Rock or Blues lick is an example of what happens if you don't block properly when using distortion. When your sound is crunchy you really shouldn't have 2 notes sound at the same time (see ex. 128, Difference Tones). Play this without blocking between the notes and you'll hear all kinds of junk floating around in the low register. Even though it's distorted, keep it free of harmonic distortion by blocking all the time. The easiest and probably best way to block consistently is to grab the string between your pick and first finger before you play the next note. But in this case, the best way to block is to shut off the first note with the side of your thumb as the pick is about to strike the next string. On the recording, the first time through is without blocking and the second time is with blocking.

MIKE AULDRIDGE:

One of the premier dobro players in the world, Mike has played on over 250 recordings by such artists as Linda Ronstadt, Dolly Parton, Emmylou Harris, Hank Williams Jr., Jonathan Edwards, Mary Chapin Carpenter, Grandpa Jones, Merle Travis, Joe Maphis, Bill Monroe, Tony Rice, and many more. He has toured with Lyle Lovett and performed with David Bromberg and Don Williams to name but a few. Mike feels that he was lucky to take up the dobro at a time when it was a rare instrument, he also plays pedal steel and that helped him get a lot of studio work as well. When Mike came on the scene the only ones playing dobro were people like Josh Graves, Brother Oswald and Shot Jackson. They were the last of the well known players from the 30's and 40's. Mike has been playing music since he was in his early 30's and never had to get a day job...he's extremely thankful that he was able to pull that off.

ALISON BROWN:

Alison Brown achieved an international reputation as a banjo player by pushing the instrument out of its familiar Appalachian settings and into new musical territory through four albums on the renowned Vanguard Records label and one on her own Compass Records. Her solo debut *Simple Pleasures*, owed much to the California based Jazz/Bluegrass hybrid sound pioneered by mandolinist David Grisman, who produced the album. Around the same time, Brown joined Alison Krauss for a successful three year run that included a place on Krauss' Grammy winning *I've Got That Old Feeling* album, as well as Bluegrass music's highest accolade for an instrumentalist, the International Bluegrass Music Association Banjo Player of the Year in 1991. Her album *Simple Pleasures* earned a Grammy nomination. Her jazz-tinged release, *Out of the Blue* on Compass, features the smooth sound of her custom electric nylon-string banjo. Together, her five solo projects represent a substantial musical evolution. For the many fans first introduced to Brown through her work with Alison Krauss, her album *Fair Weather* will mark a welcome opportunity to hear Brown as both bandleader and instrumental virtuoso in a Bluegrass setting.

BUDDY EMMONS:

The world's foremost pedal steel guitarist. Born in Mishawaka, IN, he first fell in love with the instrument at age 11 when he received a 6-string lap steel guitar as a gift. In his early 20's, he went to Detroit to fill in for Walter Haynes during a performance with Little Jimmy Dickens, soon afterward he was invited to join Dickens' Country Boys. In the late 1950's, Emmons began playing occasionally with Ernest Tubb's band on The Midnight Jamboree. In 1963, he began a five year stint with Ray Price he also released *Steel Guitar Jazz,* the first album to show the steel in a Jazz setting. In 1965 he teamed up with fellow steel player Shot Jackson to record the LP *Steel Guitar & Dobro Sound.* This led the two to create the Sho-Bud Company, which sold an innovative steel guitar that used push-rod pedals. In 1969, Emmons joined Roger Miller's Los Angeles-based band as a bass player. When not touring with Miller, he did session work for a variety of artists. He quit Miller's band in 1973 and signed a solo contract, releasing several albums in the late 1970's. After 1978, he and Ray Pennington occasionally collabo-rated with some of Nashville's finest sidemen

as the Swing Shift Band. He was inducted into the Steel Guitar Hall of Fame in 1981. In 1993, Emmons began touring with the Everly Brothers. Throughout the 1990's, he continued to do session work. Over the years he has worked with Ray Charles, Henry Mancini, Linda Ronstadt, Lenny Breau, Danny Gatton, Judy Collins and countless others adding his special sound to their hit recordings.

JON FINN:

Jon is one of the most respected rock guitarists in New England. His four-piece band, The Jon Finn Group, has performed all over the world in the most prestigious concert venues. They have released three full-length recordings, *Don't Look So Serious* (1994), *Wicked* (1999) and *Bull in a China Shop* (2007). As a freelance guitarist, Jon has collaborated with some of the finest names in music, including Steven Tyler and Joe Perry of Aerosmith, The Boston Symphony Orchestra, Andrea Bocelli, Amy Grant, Vince Gill, John Williams, Gloria Estefan, Steve Gadd, Abraham Laboriel, Josh Groban, John Petrucci, Steve Morse, Vinnie Moore, Andy Timmons and Dweezil Zappa. Jon has been a member of the Guitar faculty at Berklee College of Music since 1988 and holds the rank of Professor. Between 1996 and 2000, Jon wrote a monthly column for Guitar magazine. The Boston Pops Orchestra's recordings, *The Celtic Album* (1998) and *The Latin Album* (2001), on which Jon is featured, were both nominated for the "Best Crossover Album" Grammy Award.

RAY FLACKE:

Ray Flacke is undeniably one of the world's best guitar players. Specializing in the Telecaster genre, he remains atop the list of the most respected guitarists of the past 30 years. A native of Bognor Regis, on the southern coast of England, Flacke arrived in Nashville in 1978 and did some local gigs with Steve Earl and toured with singer songwriter Steve Young. Greatly influenced by rock icon Ritchie Blackmore of Deep Purple and the honky-tonk playing of Merle Haggard's guitarist Roy Nichols, Flacke has contributed his trademark virtuoso Tele stylings to the recordings of Marty Stuart, Kathy Mattea, Patty Loveless, Emmylou Harris, Janie Fricke, Mark McGinnis and Travis Tritt. His blistering guitar work helped fuel the success of Ricky Scaggs' early hits, *Highway 40 Blues, Heartbroke, Uncle Pen* and many others. In 1989 Flacke produced his own critically acclaimed instrumental album *Untitled Island*. Ray's enchanting composition *Tahitian Skies* was recorded twice by his hero Chet Atkins, first in 1990 with Mark Knopfler of Dire Straights, then again in 1993 with the Chieftains, resulting in a Grammy nod for Best Pop Vocal/Instrumental. The most recent recording of *Tahitian Skies* appears on

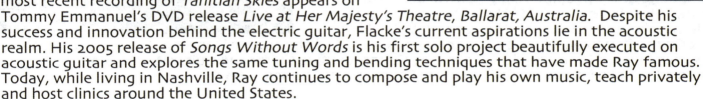

Tommy Emmanuel's DVD release *Live at Her Majesty's Theatre, Ballarat, Australia*. Despite his success and innovation behind the electric guitar, Flacke's current aspirations lie in the acoustic realm. His 2005 release of *Songs Without Words* is his first solo project beautifully executed on acoustic guitar and explores the same tuning and bending techniques that have made Ray famous. Today, while living in Nashville, Ray continues to compose and play his own music, teach privately and host clinics around the United States.

RICHIE HART:

Richie is a former student of the master jazzman George Benson and guitar great Johnny Smith. He has performed in Carnegie Hall, The Village Vanguard, The Blue Note and many other major venues. He has played at Jazz festivals in Spain, the Caribbean, Bermuda, Jamaica and up and down the east coast of the US. Richie has played with some of the biggest names in Jazz including Ron Carter, Jimmy Cobb, Dr. Lonnie Smith, Don Patterson, Jack McDuff, Freddie Hubbard and Etta Jones, just to name a few.

Richie has 4 CD's on the market under his name: *Remembering Wes* (Blue Flame records), *Timeless, Blues in the Alley* and *Greasy Street* (Zoho Records) as well as his first recording, *Just a Matter of Time* (Carat records). The release of his next 2 CD's are greatly anticipated.

He has been performing and teaching Jazz since the 1970's and is currently an Associate Professor at Berklee College of Music in Boston where he teaches courses on the music of Wes Montgomery, George Benson and other mainstream Jazz guitarists.

PETE HUTTLINGER:

By the age of 12, Pete had begun music lessons and by 14 he had settled on the guitar. Soon after he graduated from high school he went to study at Berklee College of Music, the Boston-based academic home of such musical luminaries as Quincy Jones, Kevin Eubanks, Melissa Ethridge, Brandford Marsalis, Bruce Cockburn and Paula Cole. It was there that Huttlinger found he had a knack for music theory and harmony. "All that made sense to me," he says. Huttlinger graduated cum laude from Berklee in 1984 and moved to Nashville. Since that move, Pete has established himself as a top-notch session player, composer, arranger, bandleader, songwriter and sideman. He toured, recorded and performed on television with John Denver from 1994 until the singer's death in 1997. Pete has performed on numerous Grammy-winning and Grammy-nominated projects. He has also been nominated for an Emmy for music he both composed and performed for a PBS special. His performances have been used in several national TV series, including the PBS Nature special *Let This Be A Voice*. He created the theme song for ESPN's *Flyfishing America*, a program on which he has made guest appearances. Competing at the Walnut Valley Festival in Winfield, Kansas, Huttlinger matched licks with 37 of the nimblest guitarists in the world to win the 2000 National Fingerpick Guitar Championship. He has since been featured on the cover of Fingerstyle Guitar twice, and has been profiled in Guitar Player, Acoustic Guitar, Vintage Guitar and Guitar World Acoustic. He has recorded with Leann Rimes, Faith Hill and Shedaisy just to name a few.

DOUG JERNIGAN:

From the beginning, Doug was a visionary. He knew the steel guitar was capable of being played at speeds that rivaled the other lead instruments more identified for their fast solo licks: the fiddle, guitar, and banjo. Doug was determined to perfect all those banjo rolls and fiddle riffs needed for complete tunes. He was successful, to say the least, and those skills have become a large part of Doug's trademark style. He became the fastest picking steelman of his day. That undaunted vision and his many other subsequent achievements led to his induction into the Steel Guitar Hall of Fame in 1994. In his early years ('60s & '70s), Doug toured as a backup player for Ferlin Husky, David Houston, Jimmy Dickens, Faron Young, Vassar Clements, and many others. That road work honed his skills. In 1970 Ron Lashley of the Emmons Guitar Company recognized Doug's talent and produced his first album, *Uptown To Country*. That album was one of the finest ever recorded and surely ranks in the top 50 even to this day. Since then, Doug has recorded many more instrumental albums, shared billing on others, and has been the session steel guitarist on countless recordings by such country music artists as Faron Young, Little Jimmy Dickens, Lorrie Morgan, and David Frizzell. Today, Doug tours as a concert performer, records with a host of Country Music stars and plays on the Grand Ole Opry constantly. He is one of the top 10 players in the world.

PHIL KEAGGY:

Phil Keaggy is perhaps one of the most admired guitarists in music today. Phil's solo career has spanned more than 30 years, and has included over 50 solo albums, both vocal and instrumental, as well as 8 releases with his band, Glass Harp. One of the most sought after studio guitarists, Phil also continues to sell out concerts all over the United States, with his ever-changing style, ranging from Rock 'n' Roll to fully orchestrated instrumental compositions. Born in 1951 in Youngstown, OH, the ninth of ten children, Phil grew up in a home filled with music.

In 1970, Phil's band Glass Harp recorded their self-titled first album and people really began to take notice of this incredibly gifted guitar player. In 1972, he made the tough decision to leave Glass Harp and pursue a solo career. In 1976 Phil recorded his second solo album, *Love Broke Thru* followed by a string of albums, including the acclaimed instrumental album, *The Master And The Musician*. With the Christian Music industry really beginning to grow, Phil won his very first Dove award in 1988 for his instrumental album, *The Wind and the Wheat*. Phil's second Dove Award came in 1992 for his Celtic-influenced, *Beyond Nature*. For three years in a row, Phil was voted one of the top fingerstyle guitarists by Guitar Player Magazine readers.

ABRAHAM LABORIEL:

Abraham is a world renowned bassist. He was born and raised in Mexico City where he received his earliest musical training from his father. His first recording was at age 10 as part of a Rock 'n' Roll group called "Los Traviesos." After his teen years he moved to Boston where he earned a Bachelor of Music degree in Composition from the Berklee School of Music in 1972. During that time he recorded with faculty member, famed vibraphonist Gary Burton. He traveled with Johnny Mathis, Michel Legrand and Henry Mancini and moved to Los Angeles in 1976 to begin a very diverse and fruitful studio recording career.

He has performed and recorded with many Jazz artists including George Benson, Larry Carlton, The Crusaders, Ella Fitzgerald, Dave Grusin, Herbie Hancock, Freddie Hubbard, Al Jarreau, John Klemmer, Manhattan Transfer, Joe Pass, Joe Sample, Lalo Shifrin, Diane Schuur, Sara Vaughan and Joe Zawinul. He recorded with Lee Ritenour, Ernie Watts, and Alex Acuna in a band called "Friendship" and has continued to record and travel with Lee and Dave Grusin for GRP Records. He is constantly in demand for recordings with artists such as Lionel Richie, Quincy Jones, Jeffrey Osborne, Chaka Khan, Robbie Robertson, Kenny Rogers, Kenny Loggins, Ruben Blades and countless others. He was voted by his peers in the LA Chapter of NARAS as the "Most Valuable Player" in the Bass chair for three years in a row, joining Ray Brown and Chuck Domanico in that honor.

BILLY ROBINSON:

A self taught musician, Billy began playing guitar at 10, by 15 he had his own band. His big break came in 1948 when he was hired to play with Red Foley for the Grand Ole Opry's Prince Albert Show. Not only did he work for and record with Red, he also recorded with George Morgan, Carl Smith, Webb Pierce and others. While working for WSM and the Opry, he played for artists like Tony Bennett and Kay Starr. After his time in the Army, he got a chance to pursue his love for painting and attended the Harris Advertising Art School. He became the art director for NASCO in Springfield and retired after 27 years. He now runs his own business "Robinson Graphics". Billy was inducted into the Steel Guitar Hall of Fame in 1996 and listed as a steel guitar pioneer. He has developed a technique with the 10 string lap steel that is unique. He uses bar slants, behind the bar string pulls and combinations of the two to create pedal steel sounds on a non-pedal instrument.

There aren't many people that can say they've been successful at 2 careers but Billy has been a historical figure in steel guitar and has also become a respected artist for his paintings. His artwork depicts music and musicians "the way it used to be" in the old country store, at a square dance, in a cabin living room or even at an Indian campground. He has recorded and released albums of pop and country songs stamped with his trademark sound on the lap steel.

BOBBE SEYMOUR:

Bobbe was raised on the family farm in rural New York state in grape and dairy farm country. His uncle Doug was a professional steel guitar player who traveled all over the world. He was fascinated by the stories uncle Doug would tell when he came home to the family farm where they all lived. He joined the air force as soon as he was old enough and as luck or fate would have it, he was stationed in Texas, the heart of big band western swing country. His skill with the steel guitar earned him off-duty gigs with local bands and after his tour of duty with the air force ended, he found himself working with groups such as Johnny Lee Wills, the legendary Bob Wills, the Western Starlighters and country-western great, Hank Thompson. He moved to Nashville and within two days of arriving, landed a gig with Ferlin Husky. He went on to work with Stonewall Jackson, Connie Smith, Billy Walker and Claude Gray. As his reputation grew, he caught the eye of the great Ray Price, then at the peak of his career. Ray hired him and it became a pivotal point in his life. He started getting studio work which became so lucrative, he eventually gave up the road in favor of playing on hit records. He has recorded with Elvis, Dave Loggins, Faron Young, Charlie Rich, Doc Watson, Judas Priest, Kenny Rogers and many more. He had invested well and eventually opened two recording studios on music row and began finding and producing talent such as Steve Wariner, Trisha Yearwood, Tracy Lawrence and Clinton Gregory. Bobbe continues to record and manage his store, Steel Guitar Nashville.

JOE STUMP:

Joe (also known as The Shred Lord) currently lives in Boston, but grew up in New York. Born on Sept. 18th, 1960, Joe was convinced from a very early age that the guitar would play a leading role in his life. At age 13, after seeing video footage of Jimi Hendrix, he became instantly obsessed with the guitar. At age 17, he left New York to attend Berklee College of Music in Boston. There he started to listen heavily to Jazz/Fusion guitarists Al Di Meola, John McLaughlin and Alan Holdsworth. After Berklee, he toured around in various Rock, Fusion and cover bands working 4 to 5 nights a week. He got his own solo deal in '93 and has been releasing records ever since. Worldwide, Joe has released 8 instrumental solo albums and 4 records with the power metal band *Reign of Terror*. He has done full band tours and clinic tours in Europe, Asia, Japan, Mexico and all over the United States. Guitar One Magazine said he is one of the top ten fastest shredders of all time. Joe has appeared in Guitar One, Guitar World, Young Guitar and countless other well known international guitar publications. He has opened shows and preformed with Yngwie Malmsteen, Steve Vai, Robin Trower, Savatage, Dokken, Buckethead and many others. Current projects include the power metal band *Holy Hell* and a new record with *Reign of Terror* for Lion Music/Leviathan records.

DAVID TRONZO:

Tronzo (everybody calls him by his last name) has devoted most of his life to music since he first became mesmerized by it as a youthful Rock-influenced teenager in the summer of 1972. He has literally and figuratively "traveled far" from his beginnings in rural Rochester, New York, where he was born in 1957, steadily honing his skills as a self-taught student to his modern-day evolution to becoming a world-renowned slide guitar musician and teacher. Tronzo has received the distinction of being voted one of the "Top 100 Guitarists of the 20th Century" by Musician Magazine (September, 1993 issue). In addition, the pundits in New York City bestowed their long-time resident (1979-2002) with more accolades ("Best Guitarist in N.Y.C.-1993" by the New York Press). Musician Magazine honored him with the distinction of being one of the "Top Ten Jazz Guitarists." Tronzo's unquenchable thirst for mastering his craft has provided him with a diversified taste in music, which can be seen in his unique playing style. Essentially, Tronzo envisions a style ranging widely in emotion and technique, weaving freely through all of the music he plays. The result is a startlingly innovative body of extended techniques for the slide guitar for which he is credited with creating fluid single lines, finger-behind-the-slide chords, and harmonic slaps, using unconventional slide accoutrements such as plastic cups, rags, pencils and wires. In February 2002, critic Laurence Donahue-Greene credited Tronzo as being "a pioneer of the modern slide guitar."

ARTIST'S WEBSITES

Please visit the artist's web sites to find out more about them and their music.

MIKE AULDRIDGE: www.mikeauldridge.com. On his site you can hear audio samples, buy CDs, DVDs, instruction books, instruments and more.

ALISON BROWN: www.alisonbrown.net. On her site you can read about her career, her biography and her recordings. At compassrecords.com/alison-brown you can buy her CDs.

BUDDY EMMONS: www.buddyemmons.com is an excellent place for licks, photos, info on his gear and much more. A wonderful place for all things pedal steel is at www.scottys music.com and steelguitarforum.com or steelguitarmusic.com/music.html. At those sites you can find Buddy's CDs and instructionl material.

JON FINN: www.jonfinn.com, myspace.com/jonfinngroup, youtube.com/jonfinngroup. On his sites you can learn all about Jon, upcoming gigs, buy his CDs, get free lesson material, write on his forum and hear him perform with his band.

RAY FLACKE: www.myspace.com/rayflacke has info on Ray, a blog, audio and video clips and more. You can buy his instructional material from Homespun Tapes at this address, www.homespuntapes.com/shop/product.aspx?ID=328.

RICHIE HART: www.RichieHartJazz.com. You can keep track of Richie, his tour dates and more. You can read about and hear Richie play at... profile.myspace.com/index.cfm?fuseaction=user.viewprofile&friendid=59128051

PETE HUTTLINGER: www.petehuttlinger.com. Listen to his amazing music, buy his CDs, guitar instruction books, free TAB and much more. Excellent site.

DOUG JERNIGAN: www.digndoug.com. You can buy his CDs, steel guitar instruction materials and much more.

PHIL KEAGGY: www.philkeaggy.com/index2.html. Listen to his iTunes podcasts, buy his CDs, instructional books, DVDs and hear audio clips from his wonderful albums.

ABE LABORIEL: www.angelfire.com/music/worldpop/MU110/ is an official site but if you search under his name, you'll find plenty of other sites with videos (YouTube) and background info on him.

BILLY ROBINSON: www.billyrobinson.net is his home site. YouTube had lots of clips of him performing at steel guitar shows so check those out. See www.scottysmusic.com/audio.htm to buy his CDs.

BOBBE SEYMOUR: www.steelguitar.net is Bobbe's store. You'll find instruments, video clips, instructional materials and other steel guitar realted material. Great site.

JOE STUMP: www.joestump.com. You'll learn everything you would ever need to know about Joe and his music. Audio, video, free lesson videos, tour dates etc.

DAVID TRONZO: www.myspace.com/tronzo. You can listen to audio and watch video clips of Tronzo in action. Search Yahoo for where to buy his CDs.

KEOLA BEAMER: www.kbeamer.com. Here you can purchase his online lessons, DVD lessons, CDs, learn about Slack Key Guitar history and much more.

THE WALTZ:

The waltz has been around since the the late 1780's. It started in Vienna, Austria and quickly spread throughout Europe. Today there are usually only 3 kinds of music in the 3/4 time signature that you'll have to know about. 1. The Viennese Waltz, 2. The Jazz Waltz and 3. The Pop Song in 3/4.

Here is the standard Viennese Waltz, think um-pah-pah, um-pah-pah.

a.

One of the characteristics of Jazz is the use of anticipations. If you anticipate the second beat by an eighth beat, you get the Jazz Waltz. Since Jazz usually swings, you'll also be using swing eighth notes. Even though the anticipated second beat is now on the "and" of a beat, it is played with a down stroke to accent it.

b.
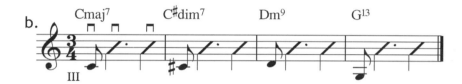

The next example shows some variations on the Jazz Waltz by adding attacks on the "and" of two and the "and" of three. Sometimes with a chord sound, sometimes with a no-tone-chic (dead strings).

While playing a chord progression, you may want to change the repetitiveness of the pattern by adding in a measure of three quarter notes at the end of a phrase. Here's and example using all of the above rhythm patterns.

c.
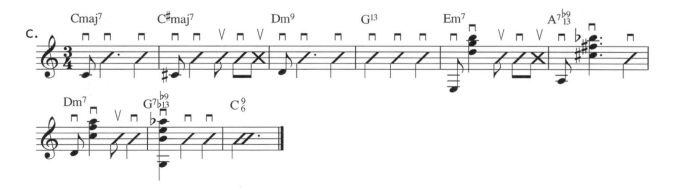

THE POP SONG IN 3/4:

Most Pop songs use a combination of a half time feel and a standard waltz. The half time feel is much hipper and has a nice slow groove to it. It's usually more like a 12/8 or 6/8 feel followed by a change to the standard 3/4 feel in the chorus. The only real difference between the two is how the drummer plays it.

Here's an example of the rhythm guitar and drum part in the half time feel section.

Here's what it might look like when they change to the standard 3/4 feel.

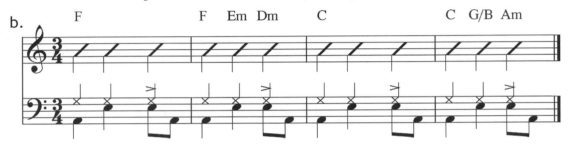

TAPPING DOUBLESTOPS and TRIADS:

Why limit yourself to tapping one note at a time? Try two. In this example, the tap is done with the first and second finger of the picking hand. In the second measure, a double note bend is followed by a two note tap. Remember, the tap happens lower than the apparent pitch because the strings are already bent up.

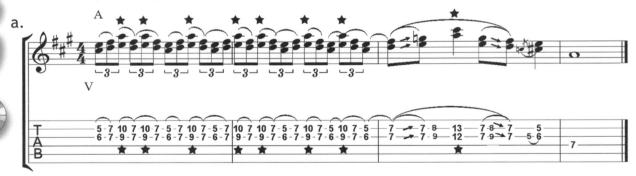

Feeling adventurous? Go for it! Try 3 note taps!
The fingering on the D^7 chord tap is Thumb, 1 and 2.

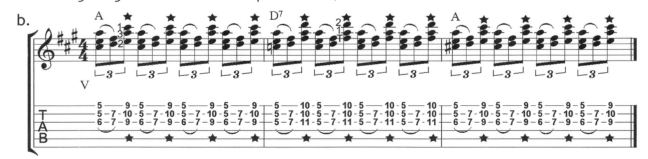

There are two types of diminished scales. One starts with a half step followed by a whole step, the other starts with a whole step followed by a half step. The whole-half is the most common variety. It can be used on almost any diminished chord you come across. Sometimes the dim. chord is actually a misspelled dom$^{7(b9)}$ chord and should be treated as such. On a sharp one diminished chord, for example, the harmonic minor scale from its 7th degree would become the appropriate scale to use. Here is an easy fingering for the whole-half diminished scale. Just remember the fingering 1-2-4, 1-3-4 and after the 6th and 5th string are played, move back a fret and stay there for the rest of the scale.
Diminished scale (whole step-half step) easy fingering.

Here is a 3 octave version of the diminished scale using a constant fingering. It's a bit awkward, but after you get used to the stretches you'll find it moves along quite easily.

Another fun Country open string lick in G. Going all the way up the neck to the classic Country ending lick. Remember to let the note before the open string ring into that open string to create a smooth layered type of sound. For example, the C rings into the open D, the F# rings into the open G etc.

192

Here's a couple of Funk rhythm guitar examples. These are the kind you'd play against a repetitive groove. On the E7#9 example, give the G natural a little quarter step bend on the "and" of beat four. Make sure your other fingers don't move when you bend it. The other 2 single line examples could accompany those rhythm parts as the 2nd guitar part.

193

A good Blues lick using tension 13 and #9. Get the pull-offs going at a fairly fast tempo and give that last Eb a little squeeze up a quarter step. As always, when you bend up a note like the Eb, you have to block the string before you release the bend. You don't want to hear the pitch go down, just up a little bit before you shut it off. In this case, the block is best done by grabbing the string between your pick and first finger.

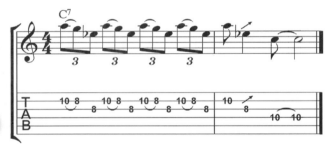

194

An Edim7 arpeggio followed by a Cdim7 arpeggio played in thirds adds a nice forward motion to this Jazz lick. This is also a good example of playing notes that don't really belong but the rising motion and parallelness of the phrase is so strong that you don't mind. On the G7 chord there's a Gb that is a major 7th on that chord, a very wrong note and it's not even a chromatic approach to some other chord tone but because of the constant structure of the dim. arpeggio, we don't hear it as a bad note.

Another great Jazz "break" lick for when the band stops and you have to play something impressive all by yourself until they come back in. In this case the tune's in a minor key so using a C#, taken from the A⁷ chord, is a normal technique. The E♭ major arpeggio is a little different though.

This Jazz lick uses an E melodic minor scale (minus the notes E and A). It's played in thirds with some skips. Another example of adding the major 7th note on a minor chord for an unusual sound. This lick also sounds good over an A⁷ chord because it makes a big deal out of the Lydian note D#.

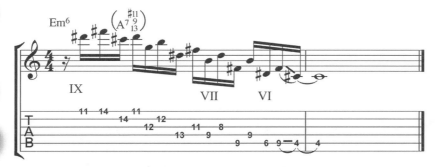

THE HARPSICHORD/OBOE SOUND:

If you believed me when I said the guitar could sound like a Clarinet (ex. 140), then you'll like this one too. Not quite a Harpsichord or an Oboe, but another new tone for you to use. In this case, pick as close to the bridge as you can. You'll hear a nasal kind of sound a little bit like an Oboe or a Harpsichord. Another way of getting the same sound is to pick right behind your fretting finger. It has the same effect as picking by the bridge but more importantly, it looks cool!

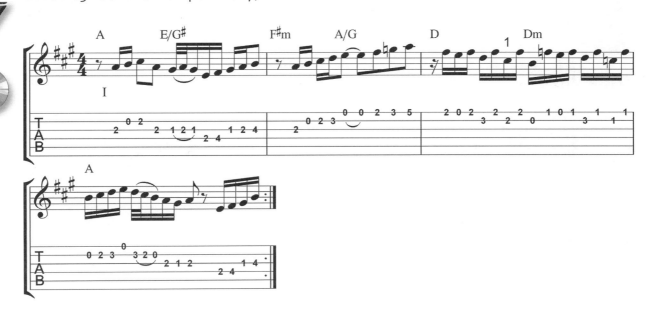

198

Here's a great warm up exercise for developing finger independence. On the first string, hold down both A and B♭ with your 3rd and 4th fingers. On the second string, play D to E♭ over and over. It is *very* important that you lift each finger after it's been played if you want to get the most out of this exercise.

III   Hold down 3 & 4, pick and lift 1 & 2   Hold down 2 & 4, pick and lift 1 & 3

Hold down 2 & 3, pick and lift 1 & 4   Hold down 1 & 2, pick and lift 3 & 4
(this one's hard!)

Hold down 1 & 3, pick and lift 2 & 4

199

+ DVD

A Ragtime style fingerpicking example. Still using the thumb-one-thumb-two pattern shown in ex. 88, this one walks up through different inversions of the chords and could be a good bridge for a tune in the key of C. Except for the first 2 quarter notes of bars one and five, let all the other notes ring out.
The written example below starts in measure 17 on the recording.

DROP 2 and DROP 3 VOICINGS:

Most of the chords we play on guitar are what's called drop 2 or drop 3. That's a method of creating chords that are playable on the instrument. The term "close 4" is used to describe a voicing where all the notes are voiced as close to each other as possible. Those are easy for a piano player to play but usually next to impossible for the guitarist. In order to make them playable, we employ one of the above methods.

This is a close 4 Cmaj⁷ chord with E in the melody...  in order to play it

on guitar, you'd have to do this... but when you take the second note down

from the top, and drop it an octave, you get this. Much easier.

Here's a close 4 Gmaj⁷ chord with D in the melody... 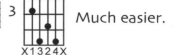 in order to play this, you'd

use your picking hand to fret the F♯. But when you take the 3rd note down from

the top and drop it an octave, you get this.

Here are a few more shown in close 4 then in the dropped version.

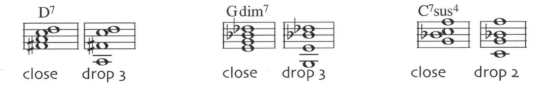

D⁷		Gdim⁷		C⁷sus⁴	
close	drop 3	close	drop 3	close	drop 2

A Motown type "slick lick." Using leaps of a perfect 4th, because of their noncommittal tonal quality, lets you use this lick in almost any style, but it sounds best in a slow funky ballad. Don't be afraid to try licks in other styles. I played this recently on a Country tune and it sounded really good.

Here's all the inversions you'll need when descending from a V chord to a I chord or from a I⁷ chord to the IV chord. Experiment with different rhythms. Arpeggiate them, slide all of them, pick all of them, be creative. This will work in Blues, Country, Rock and Jazz.

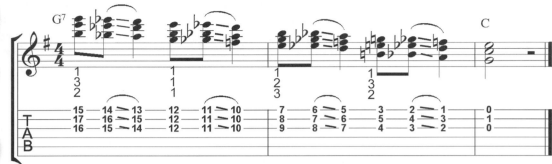

A Jazz lick that is another example of forcing notes where they don't belong. This repetitive phrase is 6 beats long so it gets displaced as it progresses which makes it sound even more interesting. The notes, however, don't always work on the chords. Analyze it, you have #11 and #9 on the C major chord, major 7 on the G⁷ chord and a major third on the D minor chord. Under most circumstances those would be mistakes but when played quickly enough, the shape and repetitiveness of the phrase makes it work.

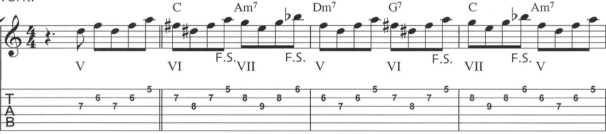

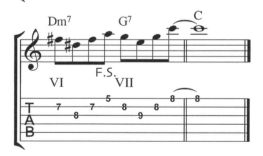

Yet another Country way of resolving 2 to 3 on a major chord, this time by bending an open string behind the nut. I think the picking hand thumb works best in this situation, but you could use your first finger as well. The C⁷ lick uses a nice chromatic approach like pedal steel players often use.

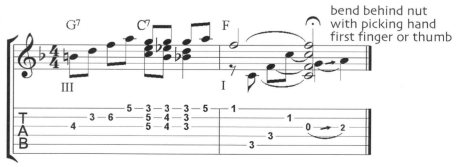

bend behind nut
with picking hand
first finger or thumb

2050 Another one of those "guitar licks" that make no sense other than it uses a constant shape as you cross the strings. Look at the shape in the tab, it's a diagonal line going from the eighth fret to the tenth, then the lick just moves over to the next three strings and keeps going until you resolve it to the high C. Start on C, end on C and who cares what happens in-between. To go the other way, start on the high C, play the pattern in reverse and resolve the low B♭ to C. This lick works in Rock, Funk or Jazz but it needs to be played fairly fast to be effective.

2060 Here is Country/Blues shuffle exercise using double chromatic approaches to the lower note of a 6th interval (see ex. 81, 82, 83 and 84 for more on approach techniques). I know that sounds way too fancy for a Country lick, but it's always better if you understand why a lick works. I've heard piano players use licks like this a lot.

Be careful when sliding up an octave. You have to time your slide to arrive at the high note right on the beat. Don't get there before the 3rd beat. The best way to do this is to wait a bit before leaving. Start your slide around the second beat.

2070 A good Jazz example using chromatics to create smooth lines, followed by a Dm⁷ arpeggio then altered 9 tensions, back up a ♭9 arpeggio and finally ♯9 and ♭9 resolving to the G on the C chord.

VOICINGS IN FOURTHS:

These nondescript sounding chords work well in Jazz and Blues because they don't sound like a regular major or dominant chord. This example takes a C major scale and harmonizes it in 4ths. Because of the notes in the scale, it's not always a perfect 4th interval, but you use whatever's available. Take the shape found in the 3rd measure on beat 3 and play it randomly over a blues progression, making sure that the top note of each voicing belongs in the blues scale. You can hear that it works most of the time and if it's not perfect, so what, it still sounds cool.

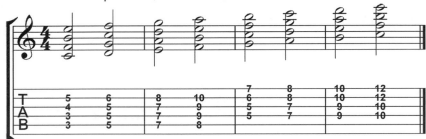

Here's an excellent Jazz phrase that takes a simple dominant seventh lick and moves it around to create new tensions. The first 4 notes make a little dominant 7th arpeggio (3, 5, 1, ♭7) on a B♭ chord, but over G⁷♯⁹ that pattern turns into 5, ♭7, ♯9, and ♭9. The actual dominant 7 arpeggios are listed above each lick. A very clever use of a parallel phrase and it's useful in Jazz, Blues and Rock. The last scale is C harmonic minor.

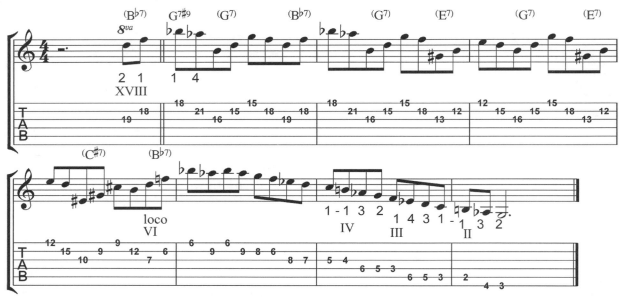

This is a real pretty Country example using prebends. It's difficult to play in tune because you won't know if you've bent far enough until it's too late. With practice, you'll get used to your own string gauges and you'll know by the feel of the strings if you've bent a whole step or a half step. The last half note chord uses a bend behind the nut. Be careful, this is the kind of lick I call the "cheese slicer."

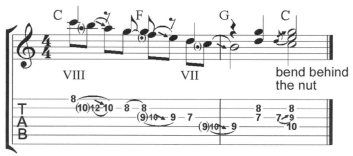

If you have your strings locked down at the nut, or if you just want to look cool, you can do the last bend by grabbing the 3rd string behind your fretting hand and yanking it up the whole step.

SALSA:

Salsa is a diverse style of music mostly Spanish Caribbean in origin. The term Salsa can be used to describe a wide range of musical styles that originated in Cuba, like the cha cha and the mambo. Today's Salsa was largely developed by the Cuban and Puerto Rican immigrants to the New York City area.

The instrumentation is driven by the percussion players. Including congas, timbales, claves, cowbell, shakere and other percussive instruments, Salsa also utilizes the guitar, piano, trumpet, trombone, bass and drums. Depending on the artist, there may be as many as a dozen or more players in the group.

As you'll see in these examples, one of the defining characteristics of this style is the bass player's pattern of landing on beat 4 and not on the downbeat of beat one where you would expect it. Making beat 4 feel more like a downbeat creates a very unique feel to this style.

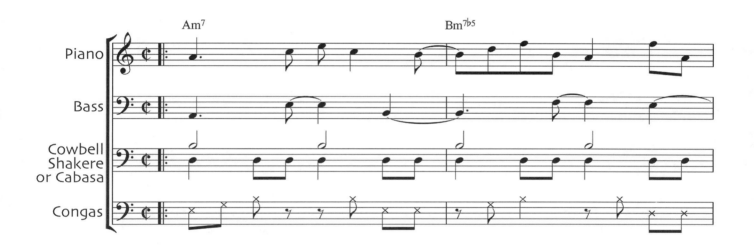

The Salsa melody or accompaniment is often triad arpeggios played as thirds. The bass will almost always hit and hold on the 4th beat of the measure skipping the usual hit on the downbeat of the next measure although after 4 or 8 measures the pulse will start again with a downbeat on beat one.

These rhythms are typical of the horn parts used in a Salsa tune. There may be just one rhythm used for the entire tune or they may use a different one for another section of the song.

Although there isn't much rhythm guitar in traditional Salsa music, when it comes up on a gig or in a session, you should borrow rhythms from the piano player. Keep it syncopated and you'll be alright. Think like the percussionist and play repetitive patterns like these.

This very emotional Blues lick is used on the I chord in measure 4 of the 12 bar blues progression leading you into the IV chord in bar 5. The notation is only an approximation of the correct rhythm. It's the kind of lick you just feel rather than count. The recording will help a lot. The fun technique here is the first bend. As you bend F up to G, you also bend C up to D on the second string accidentally. Since it's already bent, play the C (now a D) and release it back to C. Try to make this transition from the first string to the second as smooth as possible. See ex. 243 for a similar lick.

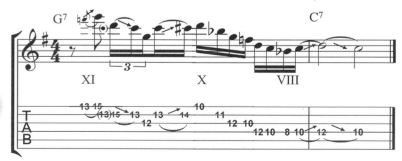

THE BLUES - A BRIEF HISTORY:

The Blues is a vocal and instrumental form of music based on the use of the blue notes ($\flat$3, $\flat$5 and $\flat$7) and a repetitive pattern which is most of the time a twelve bar structure. It evolved in the United States in the communities of former African slaves, from spirituals, praise songs, field hollers, shouts, and chants. The use of blue notes and the prominence of call-and-response patterns in the music and lyrics are indicative of the Blues' West African ancestry.

The Blues influenced later American and Western popular music, as it became part of Ragtime, Jazz, Bluegrass, Rhythm and Blues, Rock 'n' Roll, Hip-hop, Country music and Pop songs.

The lyrics generally end on the last beat of the tenth bar or the first beat of the eleventh bar, and the final two bars are given to the instrumentalist as a break. The harmony of this two-bar break, the turnaround, can be extremely complex, sometimes consisting of single notes that defy analysis in terms of chords. The final beat, however, is almost always strongly grounded in the dominant seventh (V^7) to provide a strong harmonic cadence for the next verse.

Blues has evolved from an unaccompanied vocal music of poor black laborers into a wide variety of styles and subgenres, with regional variations across the United States and later, Europe and Africa. The musical forms and styles that are now considered the Blues as well as modern Country music arose in the same regions during the nineteenth century in the southern United States. Recorded Blues and Country can be found from as far back as the 1920's, when the popular music record industry developed and created marketing categories called "race music" and "hillbilly music." This was music recorded by and made to sell to blacks and whites, respectively.

The Blues scale is a minor pentatonic scale with the scale degrees of 1, $\flat$3, 4, 5, and $\flat$7. Often including scale degrees 2, optional natural 3, $\flat$5 and 6.

The following is a very incomplete list of some of the most influential Blues artists. Please do a search on your own of these and the multitude of other great players that you should listen to:

Blind Blake, Lightnin' Hopkins. Mississippi John Hurt, Robert Johnson, Leadbelly, Bessie Smith, Louis Armstrong, Jelly Roll Morton, Big Joe Turner, T-Bone Walker, Ray Charles, Paul Butterfield, Bo Diddley, Buddy Guy, Albert King, Freddy King, B. B. King, Muddy Waters, Roy Buchanan, Eric Clapton, Robert Cray, Robben Ford, Taj Mahal, Stevie Ray Vaughn, Jimi Hendrix, Janis Joplin, Santana and John Mayer.

So I get to the gig, set up my amp and pedals, open my guitar case and find that I don't have a guitar strap! It seems my son had borrowed it for his guitar and forgot to put it back.
Thank God for Duct Tape. You take a piece as long as your strap would be and lay it on the floor sticky side up. Take another piece, the same length, and place it on top of the first piece, sticky side down. All you need to do now is punch a few holes in the ends for your strap buttons and you have a shiny, silver strap that will get you through the gig. It will also give you plenty of time to figure out what you're going to do to your son when you get home! :)

215 Here is a 3 octave diminished 7th argeggio. You'll find the pattern easy to play. Diminished chords are built by stacking up minor 3rd intervals, augmented chords are built from major 3rds. You'll find lots of repetitive patterns when figuring out licks built over these types of chords.

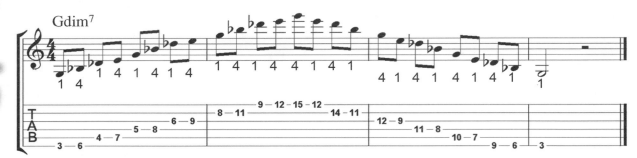

216 This is one of those Country, "Damn-the-tune's-too-fast-what-am-I-going-to-play?" licks. It's not too hard to play this really fast and it will definitely get you out of those awkward situations. The lesson here is a thing called "Pick Blocking." First of all, you're picking with your thumb (or pick) and second finger. When the thumb is picking the low note, the 2nd finger is touching the 1st string keeping it silent. As the 1st finger picks the top note, the thumb comes back and touches the 3rd string keeping it quiet. In other words, when one finger is picking, the other is muting. Your fretting hand *never* releases any of the notes, it's your picking hand that decides which ones will sound or be blocked.

217 A repeat of the same dominant 7 shape you saw in ex. 209, but this time it's played over different chords. Once again showing how you can get a lot of mileage out of a single phrase when you can use it over new chords.
The actual name of the dominant 7 lick is listed under each phrase.
The word "loco" means to play in the writtn octave, it cancels the 8va (play an octave higher than written) that was there previously.

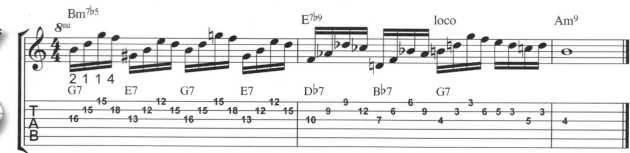

Instead of just wandering around the Blues scale and playing the same old licks, try coming up with a horn line type of phrase that can be repeated for the entire 12 bar progression.
Not only do you get to save some licks for later, but it makes you sound like you're creating a tune on the spot and really thinking about what you're playing.

These are some nice Jazz lines over a standard I-VI-II-V progression. The half notes are starting points for more lines that you should try to come up with on your own. Study the shape of the lines. Connect the dots, so to speak, and see the resulting shapes that you get.

The shape of the first 2 measures would look like this...

The shape of measures 5 and 6 would look like this...

You want to avoid shapes that look like this...

Altough smooth is cool now and then, it's not nearly as interesting to the listener as a shape that has character. Go for the skips and leaps. Mix up scales with arpeggios and chromatics and you'll have much better lines.

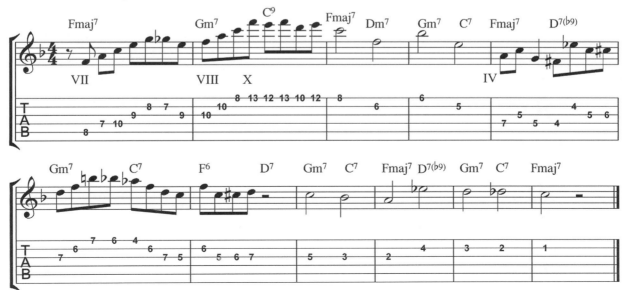

THE KOTO:

This primarily Japanese instrument has been around since the sixth century. It has 13 strings and is around six feet long, 10 inches wide and 2 inches thick. Made from Paulownia wood, which is a common wood in Asia, it is played while sitting on the floor.

The strings are all the same thickness although some players use different gauges. Originally, the strings were made from silk, but because silk tends to break, today they are synthetic. Each string has a movable bridge under it to set the tuning for that string. The bridges were originally made from ivory but current ones are plastic.

Fingerpicks are used to pluck the strings. They're worn on the thumb and first two fingers and are either square or rounded and attached to the finger with leather or paper bands. The range of the Koto is over 3 octaves from the low string to the high string. One of the most common tunings is the minor pentatonic with flat 6. From low to high...D - G - A - B♭ - D - E♭ - G - A - B♭ - D - E♭ - G - A.

All scales are a form of pentatonic scale.

The most common are...

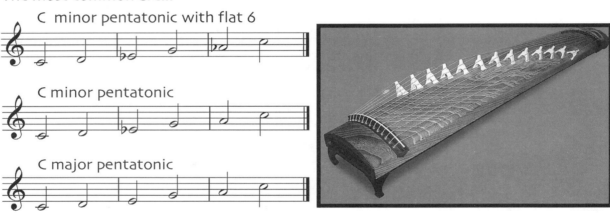

I'm not sure, but it seems to me that the Koto is the first instrument to use string bending as a regular part of the performance. As the player picks a string, they put their other hand behind the bridge and can add a little vibrato or bend the note as far as they want. The Indian Sitar uses bends quite often but in it's current form, it only dates from around the 14th century rather than the 6th century.

The most famous Koto song is Sakura Sakura (Cherry Blossom). It uses the G minor pentatonic scale with a flat 6.

To produce a sound fairly close to the Koto, I used a piece of half inch rubber tubing. Hold it in your fretting hand and use it as if it were a bottle neck slide. Be sure to block the other strings to keep them from ringing.

This Rock Ballad lead example uses the bend behind the nut trick. Check the fingering of the Cmaj7 chord. You have to finger it differently in order to have room to reach behind the nut. The 4th, 6th and 7th measures have double bends in them. In this case, play them with your 3rd and 4th finger side by side and bend evenly, moving the 2 strings exactly the same distance. The ending lick is a nice open string passage. The best part is the last group of sixteenth notes. That's where you'll hear the 5 note descending scale lick with all the notes ringing out. Don't forget to attack the downbeat of the last measure where the G is. It's the only note not held over from the previous measure.

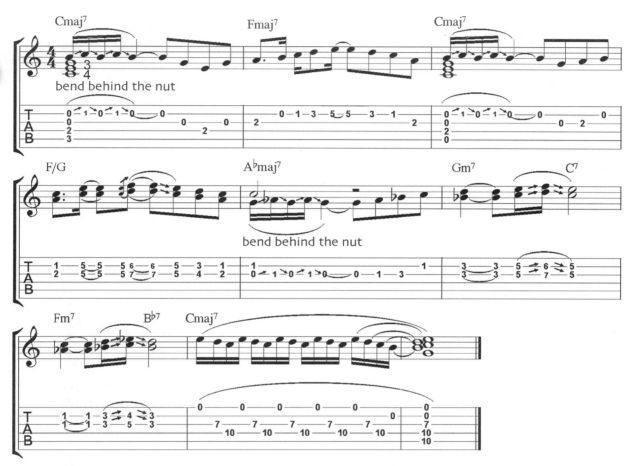

Minor7 chords are built from the root, flat 3rd, 5th and flat 7th degrees of a major scale. They are found diatonically as the II, III and VI chords. I've also included 2 minor/major7 chords. These are usually found in what's known as a "descending minor line cliche." This sequence starts with a minor chord and goes to a minor/major7 chord, then to a minor7 and finally to a minor6 chord. Songs like *Stairway to Heaven*, *Summertime* and *Michelle* use this chord sequence. It's also a cool thing to play when playing rhythm on a II-V progression. Rather than just playing 4 strums of a boring minor chord, play the minor chord for 2 beats, then one beat each for the min/maj7 and min7 chord. The downbeat of the next measure will be the minor6 chord (see ex. 32) which is the same as the dom9 V chord you were going toward anyway.

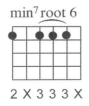

min7 root 6

2 X 3 3 3 X

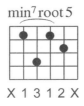

min7 root 5

X 1 3 1 2 X

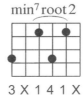

min7 root 2

3 X 1 4 1 X

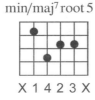

min/maj7 root 5

X 1 4 2 3 X

min/major7 root 6

1 3 2 1 1 X

THE CAPO:

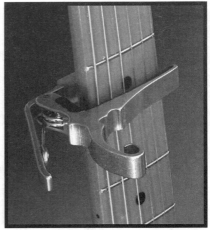

A lot of people think that a capo is just for beginning players who haven't figured out how to play their simple open chords in higher positions. That's occasionally true, but the capo has many legitimate musical uses as well. The problem with open string licks is that they become impossible to play in other keys unless you use a capo. Try some of the voicings from ex.16 with a capo above the fifth fret, those open string chords have a beautiful crystal clear quality when played in higher positions.

A capo (short for capotasto, Italian for "head of fretboard") is a device used for shortening the strings. This will raise the pitch of a stringed instrument such as a guitar, mandolin or banjo. A simple version can be made with a pencil and a rubber band. Lay the pencil across the strings at the desired fret and hold it in place by wrapping the rubber band around both ends and underneath the fretboard.

It used to be necessary to capo the second fret on a 12 string guitar because manufacturers would strongly recommend that the instrument not be tuned to standard pitch to reduce stresses on the neck. Modern 12-strings can be tuned up to pitch with ultra light gauge strings, but many players still prefer to tune a whole step lower and use a capo to play at concert pitch.

One of the more radical developments in capo design in recent years is the partial capo. These allow each string to be stopped individually and can be used in conjunction with other capos. In theory, this puts a huge number of different tunings at the player's disposal. In practice, the partial capo is most often placed either on the 2nd fret of the 3rd, 4th and 5th strings (producing the effect of the DADGAD tuning raised a whole step), or on the 2nd fret of the 2nd, 3rd and 4th strings (open A major). This requires no change of fingering above the capo. Listen to Adrian Legg and Phil Keaggy, among others, who use multiple capos to achieve some beautiful sounds.

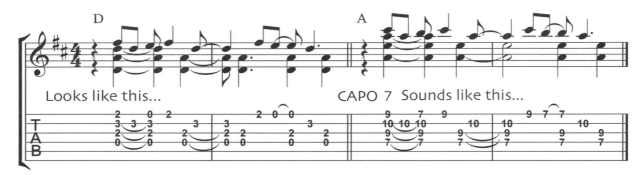

Another variation of the Bossa Nova rhythm. This time the anticipated chord rings over into the next measure. There are tons of variations to this rhythm but they all have the bass on beats one and three while the chords are played in a syncopated rhythm above them.

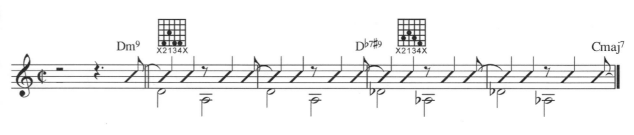

PARADIDDLE BLUES:

In the percussion world, the paradiddle is a four-note sticking pattern consisting of two alternating notes followed by a diddle, a diddle consists of two consecutive notes played by the same hand (either RR or LL). The basic pattern is RLRR or LRLL. If multiple paradiddles are played in succession, they alternate between starting with one hand and starting with the other. Tap this rhythm out on your legs using your hands in order to get the right feel for it: RLRR LRLL, maintain an even tempo. Used in many styles of music, the paradiddle is especially useful in Funk. Just listen to *What Is Hip* by Tower of Power and you'll hear the drummer using them all over the place. On the guitar they're not as common but in Blues and Country music they do show up now and then. This next example uses the paradiddle as the basic building block for the entire tune. Examine the first measure, if you look at the pitch relationships you'll see it's low, high, low, low, high, low, high, high. A paradiddle! Have fun. Pick with either all fingers, thumb pick and fingers or pick and fingers.

par-a-did-dle par-a-did-dle etc.

The dom$^{7(\flat 9)}$ chord is built from the root, 3rd, 5th, flat 7 and flat 9 of a major scale. It is the only chord that contains the most dissonant interval of them all, the flat 9th. If you play the note G on the fourth string and the note A$^\flat$ on the first string, you'll hear a flat 9 interval. Not very pretty is it? That's why it's not used very often except on dominant chords. It occurs naturally on the III^7 and VII^7 chords, and even though it's not technically available, it is also used quite often on the VI^7 chord. You shouldn't just toss in a flat 9 on a dom^7 chord just for the fun of it. The person improvising won't appreciate your hippness! The chord scale is usually a harmonic minor scale from its 5th degree. The modal name would be Mixolydian $^\flat$2, $^\flat$6. Don't forget the diminished chord forms from ex. 240, they can and should be used as dom$^{7(\flat 9)}$ voicings as well. I'm also including a few more dom^{7}alt voicings to go with ones in ex. 108.

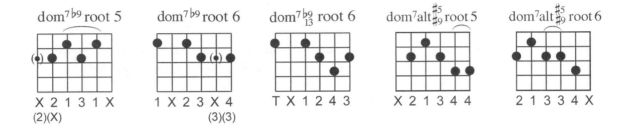

OCTAVE DISPLACEMENT GONE *BERSERK!*
The first example is just a descending C chromatic scale for 2 octaves (See ex. 43 for more info on octave displacement). In the second example, that same scale has been displaced all over the fingerboard. It's really hard to play and took me a long time just to come up with a fingering that was semi-logical. There must be an easier way to play this, but I haven't figured it out yet. It sounds as weird as it looks but I guarantee that if you toss this into some Blues, Jazz, Fusion or Rock tune, you will have everybody in the place thinking, "What the hell was that?" It's definitely the kind of show stopping lick that's worth the effort to learn. Get busy!

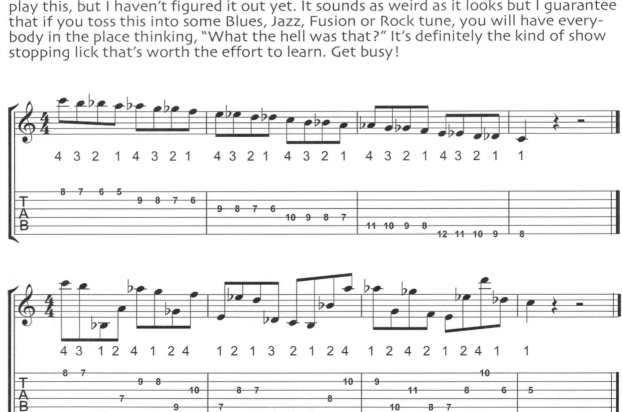

JEWISH MUSIC (KLEZMER):

Jewish music tends to be in a minor key and usually goes to the relative major key in the bridge. It can also be in a major key but instead of using the standard major scale, it will use the harmonic minor scale up a fourth. In this example of a typical melodic phrase, F harmonic minor is used over a C major chord. The clarinet is the main melody instrument. It's ability to do a laughing type of inflection adds emotion to the song. The only way to come close to this on guitar would be to use prebends and let the notes release quickly after playing them.

Here is a typical chord progression from a Jewish song. The basic rhythms are shown below. After the accents are used, the rest of the tune is more like a Country rhythm or a Polka with the alternating root-five bass and "boom-chic" sound.

229

As I've mentioned before, you should always go after the "new" note, that is, the note that's just been introduced via a new chord. The opening lick, a scale with some chromatics, is aiming for the E♭ on the Am7(♭5). It's the first time that note has been heard and you'll sound a lot smarter as a player if you go for those types of notes.

On the G9 chord I use a dominant 13 arpeggio (3, ♭7, 9, 13, 1) then just move down a fret and play the same shape. It now turns into an altered 9 arpeggio (♭7, 3, ♭9, #9) on the C7 chord.

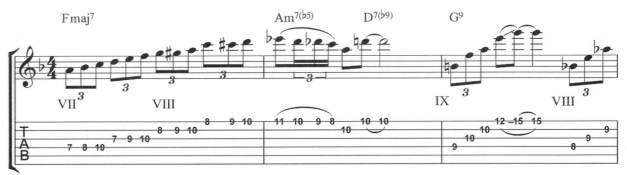

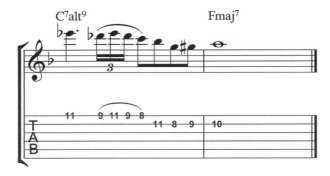

230

A Rock or Blues lick that uses pick blocking to put space between the notes. Once the A is bent up to B, release it very slowly, timing the release to reach the 4th beat. You're actually using quarter steps to divide a whole step bend into 4 pieces. In the last measure, bend the G up slowly. Don't go as far as a half step, just a little more than a quarter step and then stop the string. It's more of an emotional thing. Just give the G a little squeeze.

Pick Blocking: After a note is played, you stop the string you just played by grabbing it between your pick and first finger. This is a good habit to get into for playing Blues and Rock licks because it keeps out a lot of the extra noises that you might hear when you're playing loud and using distortion.

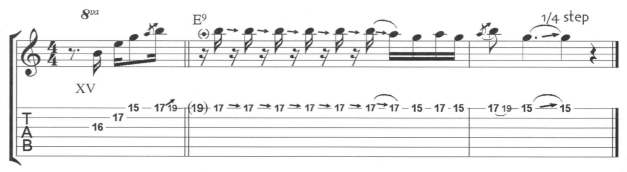

This lick sounds good in most Rockabilly or Blues/Rock type tunes. It's fairly easy to play because it lays under the fingers well with the chromatic approaches.

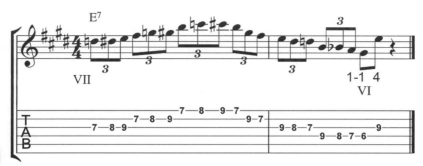

THE BOSSA NOVA:

Here it is written out for the band. You'll notice that the rhythm guitar plays the chord of the next measure like an anticipation but without letting it ring into the next measure. This gives it a very distinct sound. The bass is still just playing the root and fifth on beats one and three. That rhythm never changes. You'll get a very authentic sound if you play the rhythm and bass at the same time.

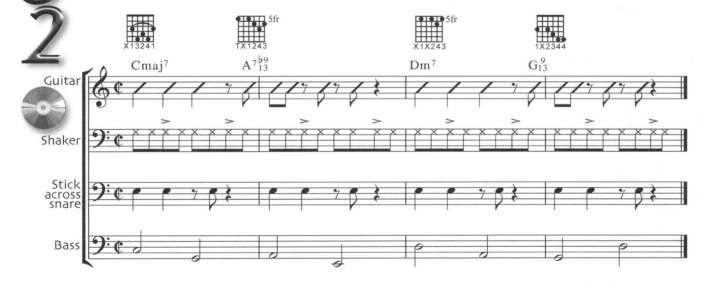

Another Jazz lick that moves up the neck chromatically. A little 3 note phrase that's slid up the neck in half steps until it resolves to the third of the Am[7] chord. Simple but effective.

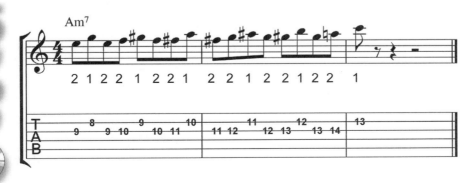

A Country example using the triple string bend. Your 3rd finger bars the top 3 strings, assisted by your 2nd and 1st fingers behind the 3rd, covering the same strings. Get your thumb up around the neck, make sure your fingers are bent backwards as much as possible then *bend them all!* All three strings must move exactly the same distance, but you'll only pick strings one and three. Yes, you could try to do it with two different fingers, but it's really hard to put exactly the same amount of pressure on two strings with two fingers. Even though it's harder at first to play it with just one finger, once you get it down, it will always be in tune.

This classical guitar technique always sounds convincing when you're trying to fake it. The basic principle is playing repeated notes on a high string while arpeggiating a triad below. Use your thumb for the low notes and your first and second finger, in that order, for the repeated notes. Try to make it as smooth and even as possible. It's not easy, but it's a good technique to have in your arsenal. On the recording, the progression continues using Dm, Dm/C, G/B, G, C, Fm/C, C.

PIANO COMPING:

There are basically 2 ways to play rhythm guitar in most swing styles of music. One is called "playing time" which means just playing quarter notes. This simple rhythm is good when the bass player is also playing quarter notes. The other is called "comping." Comping is an assortment of sporadic attacks like a horn section or piano player might play. The first example shows the regular "playing time" method. The second is the "comping" version. The third one is my own way of playing *both at the same time!* Our electric guitars are very sensitive when plugged in, you can just press down the fretting hand and you'll hear the fingered chord. It's a lot like tapping, but with only one hand. This leaves your picking hand free to play whatever rhythms you wish. You can keep it simple like my example or get really complicated. Either way, it'll add some spice to your rhythm playing. Check out the more complicated rhythms I played in my video segment.

Playing Time

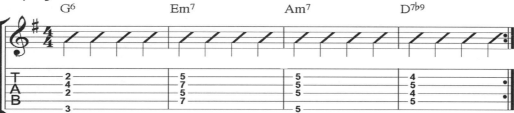

Comping

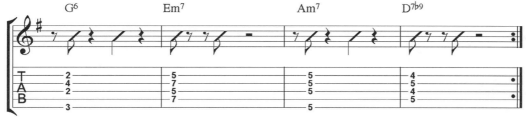

Time plus Comping

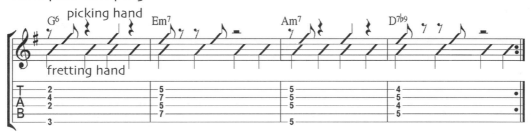

Here's a hot Bluegrass lick. This would work well by itself or when you have a break to fill up. Again, the strength of your pull-offs is critical to getting the right sound.

THE LAP STEEL GUITAR: Also known as a Hawaiian Guitar differs from a regular guitar in the way that it is played. The lap steel guitar is held in your lap facing toward you. The strings are raised above the fretboard. Instead of pressing them to the frets, a steel bar is laid against the strings. Typically the lap steel guitar is tuned in one of several "open" tunings rather than the standard guitar tuning. Steel guitars were invented and popularized in Hawaii. Legend has it that in the late 1880's, Joseph Kekuku, a Hawaiian schoolboy, discovered the sound while walking along a railroad track strumming his guitar. He picked up a bolt lying by the track and slid the metal along the strings of his guitar. Intrigued by the sound, he taught himself to play using the back of a knife blade. Hawaiian groups were a big hit at the 1915 Panama-Pacific International Exposition in San Francisco. From there the sound of the Hawaiian guitar spread throughout the United States. From about 1915 to 1930, a large number of Hawaiian guitar methods and songs were published by the major music publishers. The soulful sound of the Hawaiian guitar has been incorporated into Blues, Gospel, Rock, Country, Pop, African and Indian music.
Prominent players include Sol Hoopii, Speedy West, Jerry Byrd, Leon McAuliffe, Bob Brozman, Ben Harper, John Ely, David Lindley, Junior Brown, Alvino Rey and Herb Remington.

TUNINGS: There are probably as many tunings as there are players, but over the years many have become standard. The older tunings were more closely related to the guitar's original tuning but as the tunings and the instruments evolved, the tunings became specific to the Lap Steel. All tunings are listed from low to high. Older tunings: G major, (G, B, D, G, B, D). E major, (E, B, E, G#, B, E). C# minor, (G#, C#, E, G#, C#, E). B11, (B, D#, F#, A, C#, E). Newer tunings: E13, (D, E, G#, B, C#, E). C6/A7, (C#, E, G, A, C, E). D9, (A, D, F#, A, C, E). Bill Leavitt, former Chairman of the Guitar Department at Berklee, invented what I call The Leavitt Tuning. It allows you to play all the hip Jazz voicings without having to use any slants, C#, E, G, Bb, C, D (see my web site for more).

Most Lap Steels have 6 strings but lately the 8 string variety has become very popular. Some players even use 10 strings. Popular brands of Lap Steel include Weissenborn, Oahu, Rickenbacher, Gibson, Bigsby, Fender and National/Supro/Valco. There are also many beautiful steels being built today by companies such as Asher, Bear Creek, Chandler, George Boards, Gold Tone, Harmos, Melobar, Remington and Sierra to name just a few.

The most difficult part of playing the Lap Steel is being able to use slants (slanting the bar to obtain different intervals). There are forward slants, reverse slants and split bar techniques to perfect. Below are a few examples.

239

A semetric diminished scale is usually called a "whole-half" scale, which means it's built from alternating intervals of a whole step and a half step. The diminished scale below is the other type, known as a "half-whole" scale, it starts with a half step followed by a whole step. Over a G7 chord, it could be called a G altered 9/Lydian ♭7 scale. The lower half contains scale degrees 1, ♭9, ♯9 and 3, the upper half contains ♯11, 5, 6 and ♭7. This lick fits well in Jazz or Fusion styles or anywhere else you want a very different sounding phrase.

In the second example, notice how different the lick sounds when you start it an eighth beat later. You can make a familiar lick sound new by displacing it by an eighth beat or playing it as triplets.

G alt9/Lydian ♭7 or G dim. half/whole

240

The diminished 7th chord is built from the root, flat 3rd, flat 5th and double flat 7th (6th) degree of a major scale. It is usually used as a passing chord to get you from one place to another by chromatic root motion. Often, tunes will list a chord change as dim7 when it really is functioning as a dom7(♭9). Since diminished chords are made by stacking minor 3rd intervals on top of each other, any note in the chord can be considered a root. Therefore, each dim7 chord has 4 names. The first voicing below, if played on the first fret, could be called Bdim7, Fdim7, A♭dim7 or Ddim7. If 4 names for one chord aren't enough for you, a half step *below* each of the chord tones can be found the root of a dom7(♭9) chord. So, the same voicing could also be called B♭7(♭9), E7(♭9), G7(♭9) or D♭7(♭9). Not bad, huh? 8 Chords for the price of one!

dim7 root any strg.   dim7 root any strg.   dim7 root any strg.

X 2 3 1 4 X   2 X 1 3 1 X   X X 1 3 2 4

These chords are also dom7♭9 with their root a fret below any note.

241

A pretty Jazz lick over an Am7 chord, although it would sound just as good over D9, D9sus4 and Cmaj7. Always take the time to analyze why a particular lick sounds good. In this case, over the Am7 chord, tensions 11, 9 and 6 are used at the beginning of some of the groups of sixteenth notes. If you think of it over D9sus4, you get 13, 4 and 9. Over Cmaj7, you get 9, 7, 6 and ♯11.

On the recording I play the same lick over Am7, D9sus4, Em9, Cmaj7 ending on an Eadd2 chord.

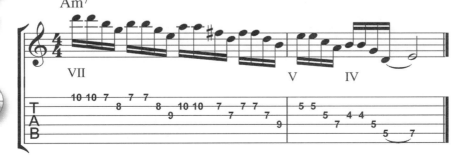

BANJO VOICINGS:

These 4 note voicings work well for getting the sound of a tenor 4 string Banjo. Don't use the fifth or sixth string or you'll kill the illusion since a real banjo can't play those low notes. We're used to hearing tenor banjo used in Dixieland tunes. The chord progression below is from *Sweet Georgia Brown*, a classic Dixie tune. The first 4 chord boxes show a walk up from the F chord to an F^7 chord. Use this on any major chord to help you get to the next chord. The 5th box is a major chord with the root on top. This is one of the most useful voicings for this style because it gives you the root, the major 7th, the flat 7th and the 6th on the first string to use as passing melody notes. Remember, think "do-wacka-do-wacka-do" as you strum, and think like a drummer, using lots of little triplet drum rolls into the chords. Use a rotating wrist movement in your picking hand or you won't be able to control the fast strums. See ex. 129 for a good way to get a Dixieland banjo sound.

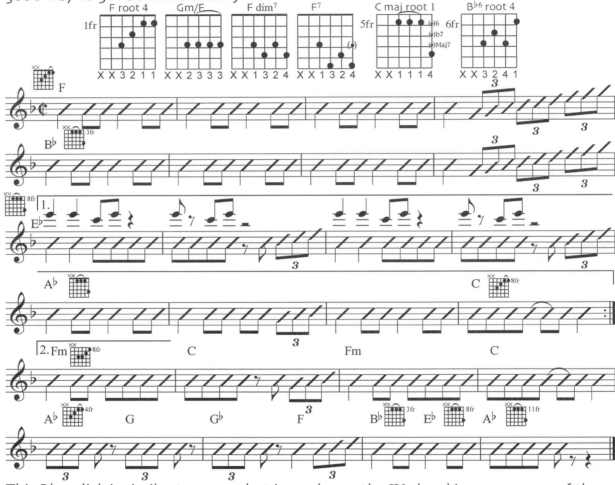

This Blues lick is similar to ex. 213 but is used over the IV chord in measure 10 of the 12 bar Blues progression. Again, the written rhythm is just a suggestion. Feel free to play it as you feel it. It uses the same fun bend described in ex. 213 for the first 2 bent notes.

244.

Fun with a 12 string guitar. Jimmy Bryant, one of the fastest, cleanest Country/Jazz players from the 50's who often played with equally amazing steel player Speedy West, had a cool idea. He had a double neck guitar, one regular and one 12 string neck. He tuned the high 4 string sets on the 12 string neck to a minor third interval. The 2 high E's were E and G. The 2nd string B's were B and D and so on. This allowed him to play his wild fast licks but in harmony as if there were 2 people playing double stops (2 notes at a time). His tune *Stratosphere Boogie* is an incredible example of this technique. Think about it, the only interval that would be right most of the time is a minor third. It's the correct interval on scale degrees 2, 3, 6 and 7 and a "blue" note on degrees 1, 4 and 5.

245.

Another 12 string technique is called the Nashville High Strung Tuning. Just remove the normal guitar's 6 strings. What you're left with creates interesting voicings with clusters in them because the low notes have now become the high notes. It's also a great rhythm guitar sound when used as the second rhythm part on a recording. It's light and airy sound adds sparkle to the overall texture of the rhythm guitar track.

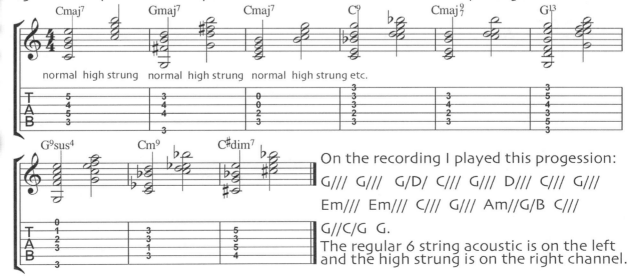

On the recording I played this progession:

G/// G/// G/D/ C/// G/// D/// C/// G///
Em/// Em/// C/// G/// Am//G/B C///
G//C/G G.

The regular 6 string acoustic is on the left and the high strung is on the right channel.

THE MANDOLIN:

The mandolin has 8 strings in 4 sets of 2, called courses, tuned like the violin (low to high) G, D, A and E. Since the strings are pitched so high, they don't ring for a very long time. This forces the player to use tremolo picking (a regular and rapid repetition of one or two notes) to give the illusion of sustain. As guitarists, we may not have the time to learn how to play in a new tuning, so we just tune it like the top 4 strings of the guitar. Today the mandolin is heard mostly in Bluegrass, Country and Folk music although it has a rich tradition in many other cultures as well. The Italians, Irish, Brazilians and Greeks use the mandolin extensively in their music.

There are many other forms of the mandolin. The mandola, tuned a fifth below the mandolin, the same relationship as the viola to the violin. The octave mandolin, tuned and octave below the mandolin. The mando cello, tuned an octave and a fifth below the mandolin, C, G, D and A, the same relationships of the cello to the violin. Although very uncommon, there is also a mando bass. It only has 4 strings and is tuned like the double bass, E, A, D and G. Mandolin orchestras decided the real double bass sounded better so they stopped making the mando bass.

ITALIAN MUSIC:

Remember, these examples are showing you the most common or characteristic licks of any given style. If someone calls an Italian tune and you play thirds and sixths with a lot of tremolo picking you'll sound correct for the style. The hardest part is getting an even attack as you tremolo pick. Some people play with a rigid forearm and pick from the elbow and others will use the rotating wrist technique (see ex. 158) to achieve this effect. The most common is picking from the elbow. On the recording I used the Line 6 Variax set to Mandola to get a more authentic sound.

THE B-BENDER:

It seems like everybody is trying to sound like a pedal steel guitar nowadays. Some of the gadgets created for that purpose are, the Bigsby Palm Pedal (2 levers mounted at the bridge, one raises the 2nd string a whole step, the other raises the 3rd string a half step), the Hip Shot (uses a lever activated by pushing the guitar away from your hip), and the most famous, the Parsons-White B-Bender, created by Clarence White and Gene Parsons of The Byrds. After carving out much of the back of the guitar, usually a Telecaster, levers and pulleys are installed to the 2nd string on one end and the top shoulder strap button on the other. By pushing the guitar down towards the floor, you make the strap button pull up in its little channel and that in turn raises the B string to C♯. They also have one attached to the rear strap button for the 3rd string. It takes the third string from G to G♯ by pushing down on the rear of the guitar. All of these complicated devices are why I just went out and bought a real pedal steel. You can come close on the guitar, but nothing can take the place of the real thing. "BB" means use the B-Bender.

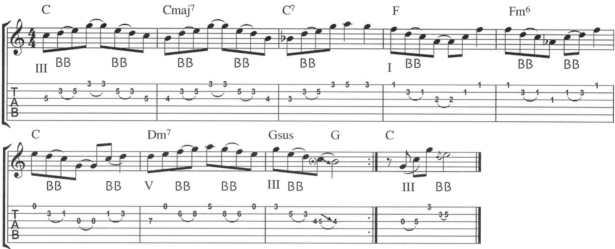

This Jazz example uses the B-Bender to grab some tensions that you'd never be able to get otherwise. You may choose not to let the listener hear the release of the pre-bend if you think it's too country, but I think it's effective when you do. The voicing in the last measure is a little tricky when trying to push the neck down while holding the chord but it's a cool sound.

The most important part of this Rock rhythm is the release points between the chords. These are indicated by the "," comma. The first chord is slid into the second one and released at almost the same time, creating a ghost note or swallowed effect, this is indicated by the "( )" parenthesis around the chord. The accented chords should be very short and attacked stronger and louder than the others. Use downstrokes on *every* attack until the sixteenth notes are introduced. When the sixteenth notes begin, the eighth notes become downstrokes and the sixteenths become alternate picking.

This open string Country lick is over an A[7] chord. You'll begin to notice the similarities that occur in these types of licks. That is, 2 fingered notes followed by an open string then repeat the pattern. Remember, the A rings into the G, the G into the E, the E into the E♭ etc. In the last measure, slide F♯ to G, hammer A to B, then slide the G and B up to A and C♯.

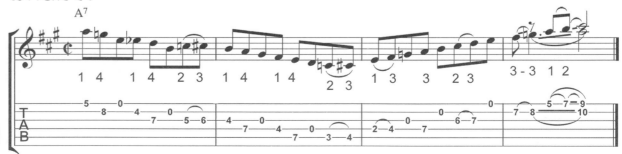

If you haven't figured it out by now, there is *nothing* more Country then having the second degree hammer or bend to the third degree on a major triad. So far, I've shown you lots of ways to bend from 2 to 3. Here are all the inversions of a V chord resolving to the I chord with all the hammer-on possibilities of 2 to 3.

They're organized on each of the four 3-string groupings starting with the bottom 3. If you can get this *down*, you will be able to improvise in triads, not just single notes.

Practice, practice, practice!

Question: Can you make a quarter note swing? Since swing is created by using a sub-division of eighth note triplets, you would think the answer is no...wrong! It all depends on when you release the quarter note. Play a few measures of nothing but quarter notes, releasing your fretting hand's pressure between each note. Listen to the rhythm of the silence! Is it setting up a straight eighth rhythm between the quarter note that sounds and the space of the silence?

If you count triplets (trip-a-let or 1-2-3) and release the quarter note on the third eighth beat of the triplet, you'll be setting up a swing rhythm between the quarter note that sounds and the smaller amount of silence given to the last part of the triplet.

This is a great way to make simple quarter beat rhythm guitar patterns swing without having to use up stroke dead strings to create a swing rhythm. Subtle but very cool.

THE CONTRARY MOTION BEND - TWO STRINGS UNDER ONE FINGER:

There isn't much that's truly new anymore. It's all just variations on a theme, or so I thought until I heard Jerry Donahue of The Hellecasters. He came up with a way of playing contrary motion bends (2 notes resolving in opposite directions). This is really hard to do, but it sounds so good, it's worth the effort. For the first example below, bend the B to C in the normal way. Then bend D to E going the other way. Now you have the 3rd string right up against the 2nd string. Play the note F# on the 2nd string. Now comes the weird part. Try to grab *both* the 2nd and 3rd strings under your first finger. As you release the bend on the 3rd string, you actually drag the 2nd string with you and bend it up to G! So the resulting sound is the bends on strings 3 and 4 resolve downwards as you release them, but the bend on string 2 resolves *up*. The second example uses the same trick . Get the 4th and 3rd string under one finger. Have fun!

An ending lick in a Blues or Rock tune. But this one has a surprise at the end. After playing the Em triad on the open top 3 strings in the last measure, bend the 3rd string up a half step from behind the nut to make an E major triad. Do it slowly to make sure everyone can hear it.

PROVING A POINT: This sounds better on piano because you can have all the notes ring using the sustain pedal, but until you run out of frets, it's fun on the guitar. Play an Fmaj7 arpeggio then continue up a Gmaj7, Amaj7 and Bmaj7. The notes get progressively more wrong but they don't sound bad because of the constant shape you're using.

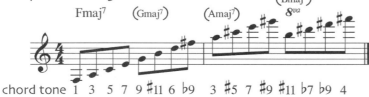

chord tone 1 3 5 7 9 #11 6 b9   3 #5 7 #9 #11 b7 b9 4

THE STEEL DRUM EFFECT:

As a kid, whenever I put the pick away, I would weave it into the first 3 strings and push it towards the bridge. I didn't know that the rest of the world pushed it towards the nut. Because of that, the first time I strummed the guitar each day, I would hear an awful sound made by the pick vibrating down by the bridge. It was many years later when I noticed that leaving the pick there and playing Caribbean type licks sounded weird and metallic and a bit out of tune like steel drums often do. Unfortunately, the pick usually jumps out of the strings after a few hard attacks. To solve this, cut yourself a piece of plastic from anything that comes close to the thickness of a heavy pick. It should be around 1/2" by 4" in size. I've found that the clear plastic CD that comes at the top and bottom of a spindle of CDs is a good thickness for this effect. On the recording, I added an auto wah and a delay with multiple very short repeats to get a more metallic sound.

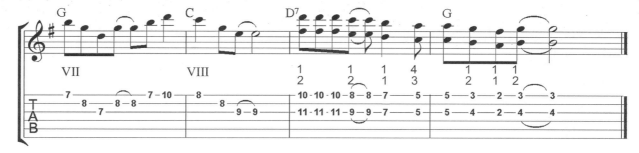

Here is a C major pentatonic scale with the addition of a few "blue" notes for flavor. Make sure the slides, hammer-ons and pull-offs are done in time and sound clearly. This lick can be used in Country, Bluegrass and Country/Rock.

The Santa Rita Connection

Peter J. Huttlinger

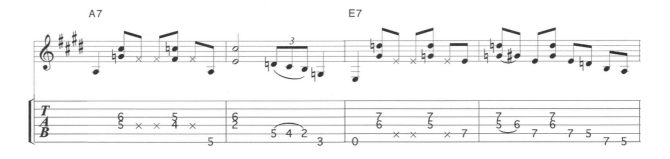

Written by Pete Huttlinger, 2000 National Flatpicking Champion.
Watch his performance of this tune and others in the video folder on the DVD.

For the rest of this transcription and many more, purchase Pete's book,
"The Pete Huttlinger Collection Vol. 1" available at www.petehuttlinger.com

2 5 8

VOICE, THE FIRST INSTRUMENT:

Singing is so basic to humans its origins are long lost in antiquity and predate the development of spoken language. The voice is presumed to be the original musical instrument, and there is no human culture, no matter how remote or isolated, that does not sing. Not only is singing ancient and universal, in primitive cultures it is an important function associated not so much with entertainment or frivolity as with matters vital to the individual, social group, or religion. Primitive man sings to invoke his gods with prayers and incantations, celebrate his rites of passage with chants and songs, and recount his history and heroics with ballads and epics. There are even cultures that regard singing as such an awesome act they have creation myths that say that they were sung into existence.

It is likely the earliest singing was a simple imitation of the sounds heard in nature. At what point the singing of meaningful, communicative sounds began can never be established, but it was surely an important step in the creation of language.

Based on the knowledge of the singing of present-day primitive peoples, a possible scenario of musical development would begin with simple melodic patterns based on several tones. Pitch matching (several persons singing in unison) might emerge next, with singing in parallel motion (the natural result of women or children singing with men), call-and-answer phrases, drone basses and canon as subsequent steps. All this could lead to an evolving sense of tonic and scale structure (primitive music often uses pentatonic scales) and the development of such basic musical devices as melodic sequences and cadences.
From an article by John Koopman (used with permission).

Over time, a culture's instrumental sounds and vocal tone always tend to match.

History aside, the point is, if you want to learn how to properly phrase like a given style of music, whether it's Blues, Gospel, Irish, East Indian or American Indian, you have to first study the vocal characteristics of that culture.

Think of an instrument like the snake charmers flute, listen to the nasal like quality, then listen to the vocal sound of the native singers, or a Gospel singer adding all those little ornaments to the melody. All of the instruments in the world were invented long after the human voice had established itself as a way of making music and conveying emotion. The people who built the instruments in a given region of the world made them to sound like the vocal qualities of the singers they heard every day.

Other analogies are Folk music: The voice is simple and plain, not much vibrato. It's clear sounding so all the lyrics of the stories will be easy to understand, the instruments of Folk music, the guitar, fiddle and banjo are all clear and plain sounding. The fiddle player uses much less vibrato then their classical counterpart. Hawaiian music: The singers commonly use a very high falsetto with an almost operatic vibrato, the steel guitar uses harmonics and a wide vibrato to mimic the singer. Rock: The singer is almost screaming the lyrics with a lot of emotion, the guitar uses distortion and maybe a wa wa pedal to recreate the vocal qualities.

As a complete guitarist, you should study the vocal stylings of as many different forms of music as you can and try to incorporate them into your playing. You'll be a better musician and well versed in a wider variety of styles.

This hot Country lick starts with the typical 2 to 3 bend but then walks down a scale above the bent note. The hard part of this one is keeping the bent note from going flat as you play the counter melody above it. Once you bend F# to G#, glue that finger in place and don't let it move until it releases the bend on the "and" of 2 in the second measure. The last measure is a good lick for any dom7 chord. Grab the G#, then bend the D to E and slowly release. Don't forget, a straight line between notes means to slide with the same finger.

The major Pentatonic Scale is made from the root, 2nd, 3rd, 5th and 6th degrees of a major scale. Since the 4th and 7th degrees are potentially bad sounding notes, some-one decided the easiest way out would be to just throw them away and avoid the problem altogether. The major pentatonic is the main scale in all of Country music. Adding chromatics between the 2nd and 3rd and the 5th and 6th degrees adds a smoothness and bluesy sound to the scale.

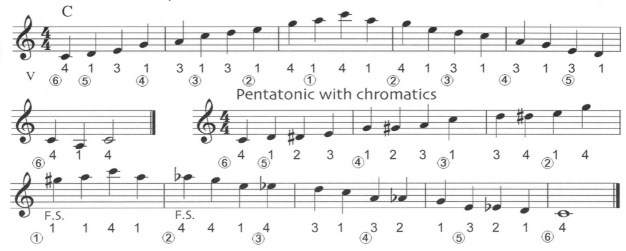

Pentatonic with chromatics

A very unusual Jazz lick that will work over any dom7 or dom7alt. chord (see ex. 318 for more about the altered chord). Dom7 chords are always the best choice to play weird licks against because they allow for so many "outside" notes. You really can't play a wrong note. This is another one of those "created by a guitar player" licks. You take the first 3 notes, played on strings 5, 4 and 2, and just move the same shape over to strings 4, 3 and 1. Then take the whole thing up a half step and do it again. Repeat as needed. I chose an E7 chord because the first 3 notes fit E7#9 but it really doesn't matter.

262

Here are some nice Jazz lines on a standard set of changes. In the first measure, the Lydian mode is forced onto the Cmaj⁷ chord for that "cool" Jazz sound, then two similar shapes on the Bm⁷ᵇ⁵ chord followed by an E⁷ᵇ⁹ arpeggio. Very smooth.

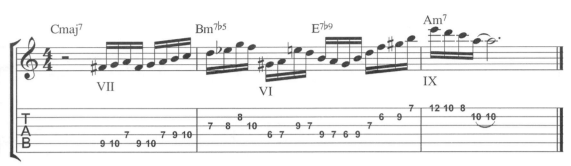

263

Tapping in Country music? Sure, why not! I admit, I haven't heard anyone else really get into it, but that doesn't mean you can't be creative and come up with something new. The "★" star indicates a picking hand tap. I suggest that you tap with your middle finger so you don't have to change the position of your pick. The G to A bend in measure 3 is done by bending behind the nut. The notation gets a little funny with taps, so I put the actual fret numbers under the tab. For example, in the 7th measure, you play E on the 5th fret of the second string, bend it up a minor third to G, tap on the 10th fret to get a C then release the fretting hand bend while holding the tap so the note resolves down to A. The last measure is my favorite because you get the classic 2 to 3 bend.

FLATPICK-THUMBPICK-FINGERPICKS-NAILS:

Depending on the style of music you're playing and the condition of your natural nails, there are a lot of options to consider other than using a flatpick.

1. PICK AND FINGERS: This is one of the easiest to adjust to because you're not really changing anything about your picking hand other than adding the use of your 2nd and 3rd (and sometimes the 4th) finger. I've always found this one a little harder than the others but I think that's because I'm used to using fingerpicks when I play lap or pedal steel. Many great players use this technique quite successfully.

2. THUMBPICK AND FINGERS: A must if you're playing Travis picking or Chet Atkins style. You can get a nice solid attack to the bass notes and it's pretty easy to adapt to. You can also grip the thumbpick with your first finger as if it were a flatpick and play single note lines so you're not really giving up anything by using one. They even make a thumbpick that looks like a flatpick that fits around your thumb to make it easier to pick single note lines or strum rhythm guitar.

3. THUMBPICKS AND FINGERPICKS: Not many guitarists do it this way. Probably because you have to put on 2 more fingerpicks and that's just something you can't do whenever the mood hits you. I happen to like this variety because I do it all the time when I play steel. Most metal fingerpicks come in different gauges. Try gauge .020.
You might also want to try the Alaska Pik or the Pro-Pik. They fit over your finger and act like a nail while still giving you the fleshy part of the finger to use for a softer sound.

4. FINGERS ONLY: This is the classical guitar way of playing. It's fine for Folk style fingerpicking, Jazz chord solos, bossa nova tunes etc., but unless you have some nails, it's hard to get much clarity out of your attacks.

5. PHONEY FINGERNAILS: If you're like me, your nails aren't all that strong and they keep breaking or splitting. Here are a few options you might want to try. The most popular method among Nashville players is called acrylic overlays. You go to a nail salon and they paint this stuff onto your nails. When it dries, it's hard as a rock. You then shape them the way you want and you're all set. You will never break a nail with an overlay on it. The one drawback is that as your natural nail grows, the overlay moves with it. Within a few weeks you have a space by your cuticle and inevitably, the string will get caught in there and try to rip the overlay off. Ouch! So you have to go back to the salon and get that space filled in. I think that wearing these overlays for extended periods of time will weaken the underlying nail so you might want to let your nail breathe from time to time.

Some players put super glue on the tips of their nails. This works well and hardens the tip to keep it from breaking or cracking. Again, I'm not sure whether the glue gets into your system or not, but if it works, what the heck.
You can also buy some acrylic powder and after you put the super glue on, you sprinkle some of the powder over it to make it even harder, then use an emery board to smooth out the nail.

A painter paints pictures on canvas, but musicians paint their pictures on silence.

2 6 5

Here's an extended example of Funk rhythm guitar phrases. This example starts off with a simple groove and gets progressively more complicated as it goes along. I wrote it this way for the sake of showing you as many different rhythms as possible in a single example. The chords with the (∧) accent should be played so hard and short that they almost sound like an "X" but with enough pitch to them that you can still tell what kind of chord it is. In the first measure, and any other time the same rhythm shows up, when you move your finger down to the lower bass note, don't move it back to the root until the next measure.

A Rockabilly example using a lot of the most common licks of the style. Remember, it's all about the sound. A thin guitar sound and some slapback echo will help you sound more authentic.
For a more driving sound, always use downstokes wherever possible.

Here's a Jazz/Fusion lick that can be used over many different chords. If you use it over a C⁷ you get a lot of altered tensions, which is cool. Over an E♭⁷ it's much more "in" sounding. You should always experiment to see how a certain lick sounds over different chord structures. You'll find that some boring old blues licks may sound new and exciting when played over an unlikely chord.

268

Basic Country rhythm guitar. Here is the original "boom-chick-a-boom-chick-a" rhythm. It works on all good 'ol Country tunes. Keep your wrist loose and make sure you can hear the first string when you strum. Often, if a student has a Rock background, they'll favor the bottom strings and never get to the higher ones. All the chords are in open position of course. Break out the acoustic for this one.
See ex. 290 and 312 for more complex Country rhythm guitar examples.

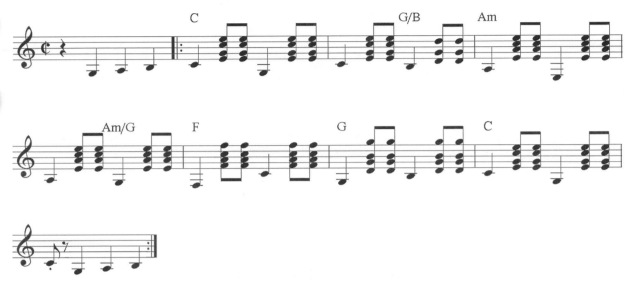

269

In this Jazz lick, the opening Gm phrase is normal enough but then flat 5 and sharp 5 are added in the second half of the measure to spice it up a bit. Next is a C^7 arpeggio up and a scale down, then continue down a D harmonic minor scale over the A^7 chord. The last II-V lick is a Cm^7 arpeggio but the addition of the C# chromatic approach to D sounds a lot hipper than the C natural would have.
Bebop scales always have extra chromatics in them. The bebop major scale is 1, 2, 3, 4, 5, #5, 6, 7. The bebop dominant scale is 1, 2, 3, 4, 5, #5, 6, ♭7 and ♮7.

HAWAIIAN MUSIC:

Hawaiian music has evolved over the years into 2 basic forms, chanting and dance. The chanting is called mele and the dance, which can be very ritualistic, is called hula. Most of the Hawaiian's music served a purpose. It was a way of passing on family stories, legends, history of the culture and praise. The music itself is fairly basic with a simple harmonic progression rarely going outside the diatonic I, IV and V chords. Even with this simplicity, they had very complex dance, poetry and vocal stylings. The use of falsetto by male singers is common and a beautiful sound.

The music we most recognize as Hawaiian has little to do with the authentic music of the Hawaiian people. It was written by Haoles (mainlanders) and was mostly cute swing tunes that described the islands and their beauty to the rest of America. Songs like *My Little Grass Shack, Blue Hawaii, Lovely Hula Hands, Little Brown Gal, On The Beach at Waikiki, Hawaiian War Chant* and hundreds of others. They were written during the 30's and 40's when Hawaiian music was very popular in the states.

If you're on a gig or in a recording session and somebody says they need a Hawaiian sound on a tune, there are a few things you need to know. The Hawaiian guitar (lap steel guitar) is commonly tuned to an open major 6th chord and that's the sound we're used to hearing. Add tension 6 to all your major triads whenever possible. Also, since they slide into a lot of the voicings, use your tremolo bar to scoop into a chord. Start with it depressed, play the chord and release the bar. Be careful, a lot of today's tremolo systems will go too far down in pitch. You only want a whole step or so. Use the bar for extra vibrato, it should be wider and slower than normal. The last 3 measures are about as typical a Hawaiian lick as you can get. They *always* end their tunes with a II⁹-V⁷-I chord progression and will either play this arpeggio pattern or one of hundreds of variations. A-loooooo-ha!

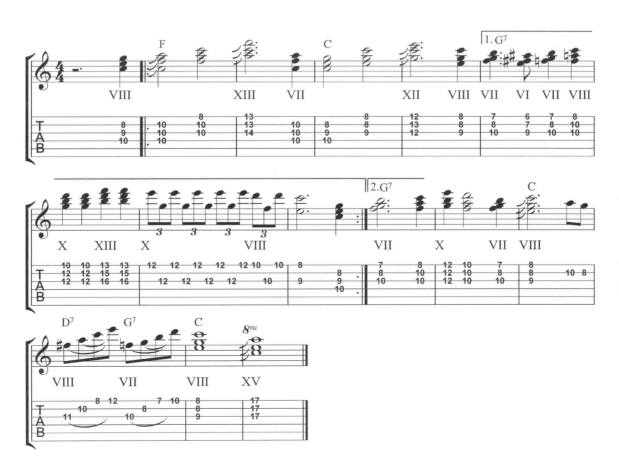

More Country 6ths. The 3rd and 4th measures are exactly the same as the first two, just on the IV chord instead of the I chord. Every semester in my Country Guitar Styles Lab, students have trouble with the last measure, so don't feel bad if you do too. Remember to lift the 4th finger up after playing the first short D on the "and" of one. Keep your second finger on the high D for both triads. Use pick and finger for this example and make sure to give the first string a little extra snap by pulling up with the second finger.

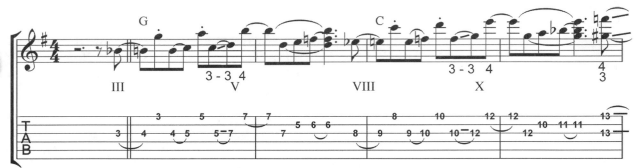

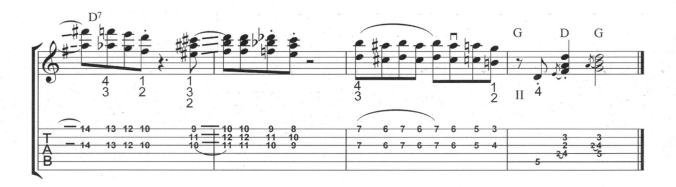

A hot Bluegrass lick. It's all in open or first position until the slide between B♭ and B natural where you change to the second position but still use open strings. It deserves repeating, make sure your pull-offs are good and solid so the non-picked notes sound as loud as the picked ones.

This heavy Rock rhythm guitar example uses mostly power chords. The second half of the example uses triads against a low E pedal. All the triads are played on the 2nd, 3rd and 4th strings. The number 2 in a circle (measure 11) tells you that the highest note is to be played on the second string. Don't worry too much about the rhythms in this part. Play the triads where they are written and just fill in the blank spots with the low E. Moderate to heavy distortion is mandatory.

Proper height adjustment of your guitar is critical for not putting unnecessary strain on your fretting hand and wrist. While seated, adjust your strap to a comfortable position, then, when you stand up, the guitar will be at the proper height. Consistency is what makes playing guitar easier. If the guitar is at one height when seated and another when standing, you'll never be consistent. Playing with the guitar way down low, although looking cool on stage, is the worst thing you can do. Over time, it will undoubtedly cause damage to your wrist.

WORST

BEST

NOT BAD

SHOW BIZ!

Never fails to impress the crowd.

275

Combining altered and unaltered tensions over an A⁷ chord gives this Jazz lick a nice sound. The first measure is Mixolydian, the second measure adds #9 and ♭9. The third measure is back to Mixo but has a few chromatic approaches and the fourth measure has #9 and ♭9 moving down to the third of the Dmaj⁷ chord for a strong resolution.

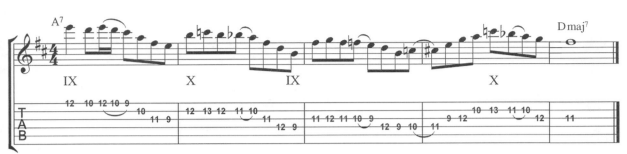

276

A simple but effective Jazz lick using an augmented triad arpeggio. Start by playing the first one from low to high then move down a whole step and play high to low. Augmented chords will accept almost any lick as long as you move it around in whole steps.

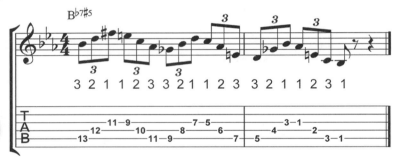

277

This fingerpicking example has a Ragtime feel to it and uses practically the same fingering pattern as shown in ex. 88. It also sounds a lot like the style called "Travis Picking" after it's creator Merle Travis. It's not as complex as the rhythms he used, but it's a lot easier to play. A thumb pick is mandatory to help make the bass notes good and strong. You should muffle the lower 2 or 3 strings to help separate the 2 rhythms. Your picking hand's 2nd finger is usually stuck playing the second string in this pattern. Try adding in the first string now and then to make a more interesting melody.

Here are 2 other voicings that work well in this style.

IRISH MUSIC:

Historically, a lot of the music that became our Folk, Country and Bluegrass music came to America with the Irish, Scottish and English immigrants as their native music. Irish music tended to be fiddle tunes or melodies played on a button accordion or a concertina. Other traditional instruments include the flute, tin whistle, uilleann pipes (a complex form of the bagpipes), harp, bodhran (a single goatskin head drum), and to a lesser degree, banjo and guitar. Although there are many different types of dance music, the ones you'll most likely run into on a gig are either Jigs or Reels. This example is of a Jig. Jigs are always in either 6/8 or 12/8. Melodically they often use triad arpeggios with connecting scale passages. A scale in thirds is a common melodic device. A characteristic phrasing technique is found on the second line, third measure. The grace note from above (B to A) is used frequently and it's not an easy lick to get comfortable with, but it makes the melody sound more authentic. Use it sparingly. Think of *The Irish Washer Woman* to help you get the tempo.

The other most common type of Irish dance music is the Reel. Both Jigs and Reels are very simple harmonically. The chord progressions are usually diatonic with an occasional use of an inversion (chord over a chord-tone bass note). You may see a II^7 chord now and then but most of the time they stay within the key. Melodically, as in the Jig, triad arpeggios and grace notes from above are used. They often use a triplet figure in every other measure. When you're trying to make one up on a gig so somebody's kid can come up and do a "step dance," the most important thing to get right is the tempo. If you play it too slow or too fast, they can't dance to it and that makes you look bad. Nobody's really going to care if you don't know a particular tune. They just want you to play at the right tempo and it's a plus if it happens to sound authentic.

CLASSICAL MUSIC:

There will undoubtedly be times when someone wants you to play something that sounds like classical music. Most of us don't have a huge repertoire of legit classical music at our fingertips, so you need to be able to fake it convincingly. You'll need these ingredients:

1. Open chord voicings (see ex. 76 for more info).
2. Inverted chord forms, or chords having bass notes other than the root.
3. Passing chords, usually with the 3rd in the bass.
4. A simple melody to go with these chords.

Add these ingredients together, use fingers only, bring out your gut string guitar and put the guitar on your left leg while seated and you should be able to get through the gig unscathed.

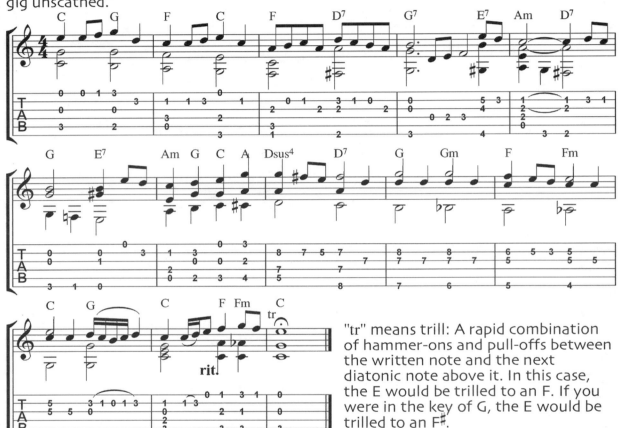

"tr" means trill: A rapid combination of hammer-ons and pull-offs between the written note and the next diatonic note above it. In this case, the E would be trilled to an F. If you were in the key of G, the E would be trilled to an F♯.

A good Jazz lick with a solid melody created by leaping from the scale passages up to the notes that resolve or connect the chords. This is followed by an Fmaj7 arpeggio ending with a pretty hammer-on and pull-off figure. In the last measure, it's a challenge to have all the notes sound at equal volume and a technique you should spend extra time with. It's very important to be able to hammer-on and pull-off without losing any of the notes.

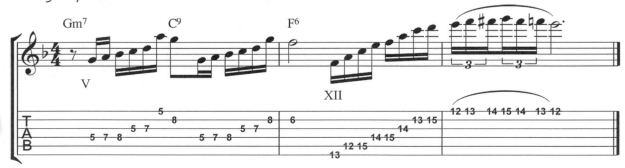

Funk rhythm guitar comes in 3 basic flavors. One is a constant repeating pattern like you'll hear in a James Brown tune, the second is playing all the sixteenth notes in the measure with occasional accents often found in Pop, Funk and Disco. The third type (like the example below) is sporadic horn type attacks. This is harder to play because you have to be really locked in to the groove.

What's the funkiest sixteenth note? The last sixteenth of the fourth beat in a measure. Practice playing *only* that last sixteenth. Listen to groups like *Tower of Power* and try to play the horn hits.

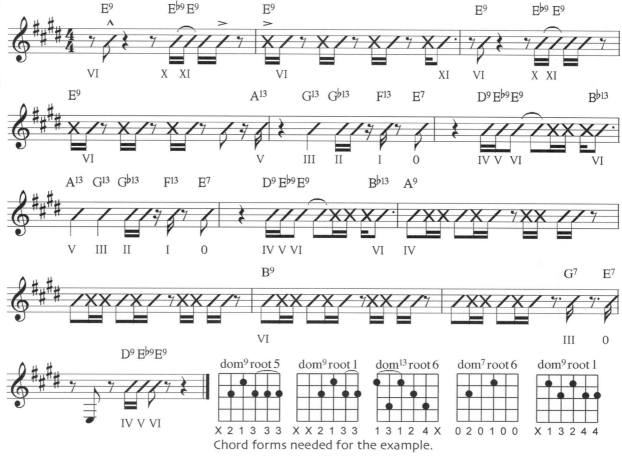

Chord forms needed for the example.

A nice Rockabilly or Blues lick descending down in thirds. The second measure has a good tritone lick, then the classic 13 plus ♯9 lick in the next to last measure but as it rings into the A chord, it becomes ♭7 and 3. That lick is usually inverted with the ♯9 note on top, but like all licks, the more you can change them around, the more licks you'll have to use.

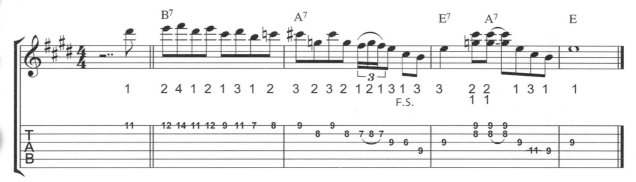

This Blues shuffle rhythm looks a lot more complicated than it really is. Once you get the first 2 measures figured out, the rest of the example just moves that pattern around to the IV and V chords. See ex. 80 for the proper fretting hand position for this exercise. Playing the low G with your thumb may be difficult for you at first, but once you get used to it, it's really the only way you can have your fingers free enough to play the upper rhythm. At the D^7 chord in measure 9 there's an asterisk, it's for what I call "The Gatton Flutter." I saw Danny Gatton (one of the most unique guitarists ever!) use this technique a lot as an alternative to tremolo picking. Turn your wrist over until the left edge of your middle finger is resting on the strings. Move it back and forth as fast as you can to create a flutter or tremolo effect. It's a great technique for getting the sound of tremolo picking without the harshness of using the pick.

* Use the "Gatton Flutter"

Snap notes with the
thumb and first finger

REGGAE:

Reggae originated in and is mostly associated with Jamaican music. Sub-genres include ska and rocksteady. Reggae has 2 basic styles: roots Reggae and dancehall Reggae which evolved in the late 70's.

In the 70's and 80's, Reggae was associated with the Rastafari movement and this influenced many of the writers and musicians. Even so, the lyrical content of Reggae music contains topics as diverse as sexuality, broad social commentary and love.

Although the bass part can be very complex and syncopated, the guitar part is really pretty boring. Just hit a chord on 2 and 4 in every measure. Since a lot of Reggae has a half time feel, 2 and 4 end up feeling like the upbeat of each beat. A fairly high voicing is best and you should usually use an upstroke to get a good clean chop. In the second part of the example I used a double chop just to show one of the options you can use. The feel for this style is a half time swing meaning the sixteenth notes have a swing feel to them. I didn't notate all the percussion, but add timbales, cow bell etc. sporadically here and there.

GOSPEL MUSIC:

Gospel is a form of religious music that grew out of the African American churches in the early 1900's. Some performers never left the church setting to sing in the secular world but others, like Amy Grant, Aaron Neville and Al Green, have included Gospel songs in their regular concert line up. Gospel may have come to prominence in America, but has since spread throughout the world.

Unlike Country or Rock, it's not easy to say that Gospel music has any specific kind of musical cliches. Some songs are double time and exciting and some are very slow and pensive but all praise the Lord and testify to the singer's devotion. Often, what would be considered a Blues or a Country tune becomes a Gospel tune just because of the lyrics. Certain chord progressions, like the one below, are very typical of the slow powerful Gospel tunes. Usually played with piano as the main instrument, organ, bass, drums and sometimes guitar would round out the band. To make the performance bigger and more church like, there would often be a choir (usually female) that enters towards the end of the song to allow it to build to an emotional climax. The wavy line pointing downward means to do a strum from the high strings to the low strings in a deliberate manner starting just before the beat, like a grace note. The chord forms needed for this example are shown in order of appearance under the example. Not every voicing is shown, only the ones you might not know because they're a little different.

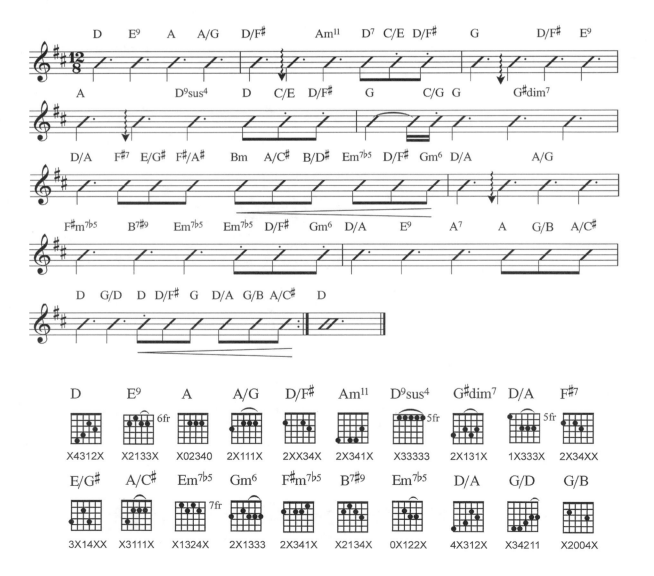

TUNING THE GUITAR (without and electronic tuner):

Yeah, yeah, yeah, you know how to tune your guitar, so skip this one if you want. But, if you don't know how to tune with harmonics or set your intonation, read on.

STANDARD TUNING METHOD:

First, let's talk about the concept of "beats." When 2 notes are almost in tune, you'll hear beats. They sound a little like a vibrato. The slower the beats, the closer you are to being in tune. The faster the beats the further away you are from being in tune. If you're having trouble deciding whether your above or below the correct pitch, drastically detune the string you're trying to tune. Then you'll know that you have raise the pitch up to get it in tune. As you tighten the string and get closer to the correct pitch, you'll hear these beats get slower and slower until they go away completely. Now the 2 strings are in tune with each other. The beats can be heard more clearly if you use distortion, although that's not really recommended.

a. Start by getting a note from a tuning fork (an A or E) or pitch pipe (pitch pipes are not recommended because it can change pitch with changes in the weather). Let's say you have an A fork. Play the harmonic on the 12th fret of the 5th string and match it to the note from the fork (see ex. 310 for more info on how to hear the tuning fork). The 5th string is now in tune, don't touch it again!

b. Play the note on the 5th fret of the 6th string and match it to the open 5th string.

c. Play the note on the 5th fret of the 5th string and match the open 4th string to it.

d. Play the note on the 5th fret of the 4th string and match the open 3rd string to it.

e. Play the note on the 4th fret of the 3rd string and match the open 2nd string to it.

f. Play the note on the 5th fret of the 2nd string and match the open first string to it.

TUNING WITH HARMONICS (preferred):

a. Get a note from the fork as in the previous tuning method and tune the 5th string to it.

b. Play the harmonic on the 5th fret of the 6th string and match it to the harmonic on the 7th fret of the 5th string. Listen for the beats and make sure they stop beating.

c. Play the harmonic on the 5th fret of the 5th string and match the harmonic on the 7th fret of the 4th string to it.

d. Play the harmonic on the 5th fret of the 4th string and match the harmonic on the 7th fret of the 3rd string to it.

e. Because of the guitar's tuning, you can't do the next string the same way. Play the harmonic on the 7th fret of the 6th string and match the open 2nd string to it.

f. Play the harmonic on the 7th fret of the 5th string and match the open 1st string to it.

No matter which method you use, you should check some voicings and see if they sound in tune. Play these next two voicings and listen to make sure you don't hear any beats.

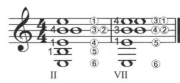

ADJUSTING THE GUITAR'S INTONATION:

The 12th fret harmonic is the exact center of a string. That pitch should be precisely the same as the fretted note on the 12th fret. Before you begin, put a new set of strings on your guitar, you can't make important adjustments with old dead strings. If the fretted note on the 12th fret sounds sharp to the harmonic, you need to make the string longer. If the fretted note sounds flat to the harmonic, you need to make the string shorter. This is accomplished by moving the saddle on the bridge either towards the neck (shorter) or away from the neck (longer). It's easy to do and if you don't trust your ears, this is one of those times when an electronic tuner will come in handy. There's no need to bring your axe to a repair shop and have the guy "set it up" when you can do most of it yourself. Besides, it saves you a bunch of money which you can use to buy more gadgets.

This Country rhythm guitar example is a little more complicated than ex. 268. I've added some hammers to make it sound more interesting. You'll notice that the hammered notes are from scale degree 2 to 3 on the chord. You can't get more Country than that! See ex. 312 for more.

A challenging Country lick using the prebend. After prebending a whole step from D to E, you release the bend halfway to E♭. Hold the E♭ into the next measure then release it the rest of the way to D. Try to keep the prebend in tune over the barline and keep it ringing into the second measure. Finally, release the E♭ to D while sliding the first finger from A to B♭.

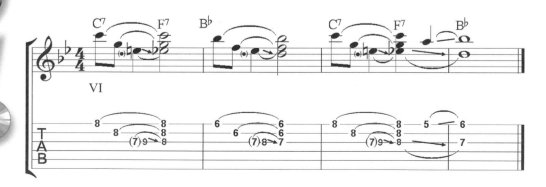

BLUEGRASS BANJO:

Using a piece of electrical wire, described in ex. 2, your guitar will sound much more like a banjo than without it. This example is a take off on the banjo classic *Foggy Mountain Breakdown* by Flatt and Scruggs. The chord progression is the same but the licks are just approximations of the very complicated picking pattern that the banjo player would use. Try this with a thumb pick and fingers or all fingers. It's practically impossible to play with a pick at this tempo.

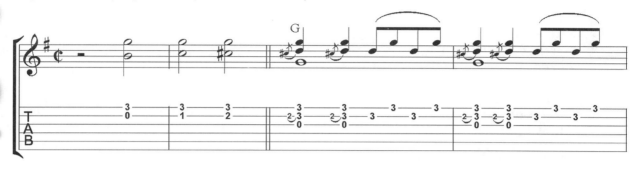

ROCK 'n' ROLL - A BRIEF HISTORY:

Originally called Rhythm and Blues (R&B), Rock 'n' Roll first started in the late 1940's as part of the African American culture. One of the earliest forms of Rock 'n' Roll was Rockabilly which was a mixture of Jazz, boogie woogie and Blues with some traditional Folk, Country and Western and Gospel thrown in. The word "rocking" came from Gospel music and meant a form of spiritual rapture experienced by the congregation during the service. Later, it gained the duel meaning of dancing and sex.

A lot of the first recorded Rock 'n' Roll tunes were covers of blues tunes but as time went by, players started writing their own songs. In the 60's, tunes by legendary blues artists like Robert Johnson and Skip James became the inspiration for groups like Cream, Led Zeppelin and others.

Alan Freed, a DJ in Cleveland, Ohio, was playing this new R&B music in 1951 and is said to have coined the term Rock 'n' Roll. He worked at station WJW and organized the first Rock concert called, "The Moondog Coronation Ball" on March 21, 1952. The event was a huge success attended by mostly African Americans. Freed put on many more of these shows attended by blacks as well as whites and spread this new Rock 'n' Roll music to larger and larger audiences.

It's a popular belief that Elvis Presley's *That's Alright Mama* (Sun Records 1954) was the first Rock 'n' Roll recording but Freed's concerts had been rockin' the crowds for years before then. In 1954, Bill Haley and the Comets topped the Billboard main sales and airplay charts with *Rock Around The Clock* and that opened the door for all the groups and artists that followed. Artists like Perry Como and Patti Page, who had been on the top of the charts in the early 50's, found it hard to regain that position after Rock 'n' Roll took off. Other ground breakers from the early days were Little Richard with his Gospel based hollering, Jerry Lee Lewis banging on the piano with his feet and other outrageous showman.

By the late 50's, Jerry Lee Lewis and Buddy Holly had gone to Australia and Bill Haley went to Europe. Rock 'n' Roll had officially started to take over the world.

At the start of the 1960's, instrumental dance music was very popular. Hits such as *Apache,* by The Shadows, *Telstar,* by The Tornados, *Walk Don't Run,* by The Ventures and *Rebel Rouser,* by Duane Eddy were topping the charts.

In 1964 The Beatles landed on American soil and music hasn't been the same since. They changed it all.

Rock 'n' Roll has plenty of sub-groupings of style from Alternative Rock to Yacht Rock (whatever that is!) and include such other styles as Blues Rock, Country Rock, Glam Rock, Grunge, Jam Rock, Death Metal, Punk, Psychobilly, Southern Rock, Surf Rock and too many more to mention. Most styles of music have a few sub-genres but Rock has hundreds.

MUSICIAN'S TIME VS. REAL TIME: I was the arranger on an album that turned out to be a really big production. I had finished recording the string section on 7 tunes (20 players in the studio at the same time!) and the mix was about to happen. I was feeling pretty good about all the work I had done. The artist told me, "The mix will be Wednesday at 2 a.m." I said, "See you then," and went home. I returned to the studio at the appointed time only to find the place dark and locked up tight. Come Thursday morning, I called him and asked him where he had been. He said he was there and the mix went well but wished I had been there too. I told him I *was* there at 2 a.m. Wednesday, but he meant...really early Wednesday morning...or as every musician in the world would have called it, "2 a.m. *Tuesday* night!" Needless to say, I didn't like the mix, you could hardly hear the strings.

Heard melodies are sweet, but those unheard are sweeter.

Here's a list of what some consider to be the top 100 Rock guitar solos ever recorded:

Led Zeppelin - Stairway to Heaven
Van Halen - Eruption
Lynyrd Skynyrd - Freebird
Pink Floyd - Comfortably Numb
Jimi Hendrix - All Along the Watchtower
Guns N' Roses - November Rain
Metallica - One
Eagles - Hotel California
Black Sabbath - Crazy Train
Cream - Crossroads
Jimi Hendrix - Voodoo Child
Chuck Berry - Johnny B. Goode
Stevie Ray Vaughan - Texas Flood
Derek and the Dominos - Layla
Deep Purple - Highway Star
Led Zeppelin - Heartbreaker
Eric Johnson - Cliffs of Dover
Jimi Hendrix - Little Wing
Pantera - Floods
Queen - Bohemian Rhapsody
Pink Floyd - Time
Dire Straits - Sultans of Swing
Rage Against The Machine - Bulls on Parade
Metallica - Fade to Black
Jethro Tull - Aqualung
Nirvana - Smells Like Teen Spirit
Stevie Ray Vaughan - Pride and Joy
Ozzy Ozborne - Mr. Crowley
Steve Vai - For the Love of God
Joe Satriani - Surfing With the Alien
Ted Nugent - Stranglehold
Jimi Hendrix - Machine Gun
B.B King - The Thrill Is Gone
Radiohead - Paranoid Android
Pantera - Cemetery Gates
Yngwie Malmsteen - Black Star
Guns N' Roses - Sweet Child O' Mine
Led Zeppelin - Whole Lotta Love
Neil Young - Cortez the Killer
Steely Dan - Reelin' in the Years
Queen - Brighton Rock
Beatles - While My Guitar Gently Weeps
ZZ Top - Sharp Dressed Man
Pearl Jam - Alive
Doors - Light My Fire
Van Halen - Hot for Teacher
Allman Brothers Band - Jessica
Rolling Stones - Sympathy for the Devil
Santana - Europa
Kiss - Shock Me

Ozzie Ozborne - No More Tears
Jimi Hendrix - Star-Spangled Banner
Led Zeppelin - Since I've Been Loving You
Smashing Pumpkins - Geek USA
Joe Satriani - Satch Boogie
Black Sabbath - War Pigs
Pantera - Walk
Eric Clapton - Cocaine
Kinks - You Really Got Me
Frank Zappa - Zoot Allures
Metallica - Master of Puppets
Pink Floyd - Money
Red Hot Chili Peppers - Scar Tissue
Prince - Little Red Corvette
Allman Brothers - Blue Sky
Iron Maiden - The Number of the Beast
Michael Jackson with Eddie Van Halen - Beat It
Yes - Starship Trooper
Beatles - And Your Bird Can Sing
Jimi Hendrix - Purple Haze
Funkadelic - Maggot Brain
Aerosmith - Walk This Way
Phish - Stash
Deep Purple - Lazy
The Who - Won't Get Fooled Again
Neil Young - Cinnamon Girl
Alice In Chains - Man in the Box
Grateful Dead - Truckin'
Van Halen - Mean Street
AC-DC - You Shook Me All Night Long
The Velvet Underground - Sweet Jane
King Crimson - 21st Century Schizoid Man
Stevie Ray Vaughan - Scuttle Buttin'
UFO - Lights Out
David Bowie - Moonage Daydream
Allman Brothers Band - Whipping Post
Johnny Winter - Highway 61 Revisited
Steely Dan - Kid Charlemagne
Rage Against the Machine - Killing in the Name
Eric Clapton - Let It Rain
Creedence Clearwater - Heard It Through the Grapevine
Stray Cats - Stray Cat Strut
The Doors - The End
Rush - Working Man
Pearl Jam - Yellow Ledbetter
Rolling Stones - Honky Tonk Woman
Judas Priest - Beyond the Realms of Death
Dream Theater - Under a Glass Moon
Jeff Beck - 'Cause We've Ended as Lovers
Bon Jovi - Wanted Dead or Alive

Natural harmonics exist 12 frets above all notes. How you play them can vary between "natural harmonics" (see ex. 35, 96, 133, 134, 135, 136), "fingered harmonics" (see ex. 159 and 160), "pinch harmonics" (see ex. 166), "palm harmonics" (see ex. 299) or in this case, "tapped harmonics" (see ex. 170 and 171 for more). It works best when all the notes in your chord are on one fret but two frets will work almost as well. In this example I stayed with one and two fret spreads. This is in a Latin style but the technique works equally well in many other styles. Although you can use any finger you want, I think hitting the strings with your ring finger works best, it seems to be stronger and attacks the strings at a flatter angle.

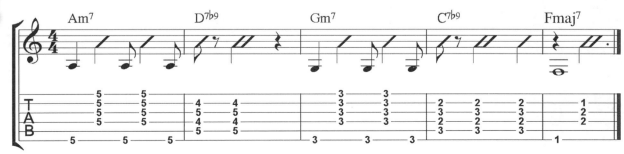

Here's another example of my slap bass technique (see ex. 127 and 332 for more). This one is a medium fast, half time Funk feel, with a swing groove. As before, most of the fingerings are based around the first finger of your fretting hand. This leaves your other fingers free to slap the strings each time you see the large **X** in the middle of the staff. The smaller **x**'s are regular dead notes played by lifting up just enough on a single note to cause it to sound dead when snapped by your picking fingers.

The last measure has a double string prebend in it. It's always difficult to get these in tune because you don't know if you're right until it's too late, but you'll get used to it if you practice enough.

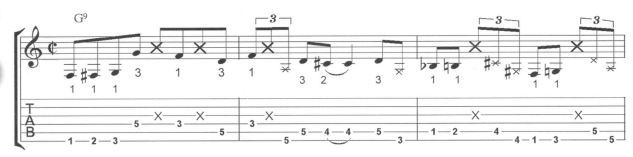

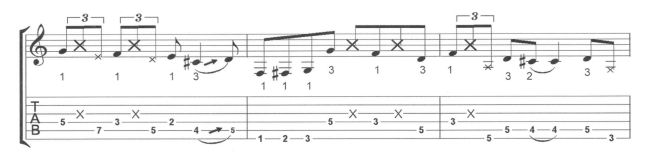

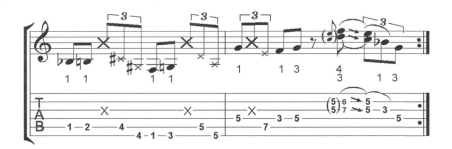

This one can work in Rock or Country. It sounds like you're playing really fast, but most of the work is done with the pull-offs. Make sure your picking is even and the pull-offs are clear and strong.

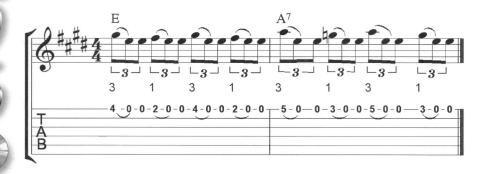

SLACK KEY GUITAR - A BRIEF HISTORY:

Hawaiian slack key guitar (ki ho'alu) is truly one of the great acoustic guitar traditions in the world. Ki ho'alu, which literally means "loosen the key" is the Hawaiian language name for the solo fingerpicked style unique to Hawaii. In this tradition, the strings are "slacked" to produce many different tunings, which usually contain a major chord, or a chord with a major 7th or a 6th note in it. Many Hawaiian songs and slack key guitar pieces reflect themes like stories of the past and present and people's lives. But it is the tropical surroundings of Hawaii, with its oceans, volcanoes and mountains, waterfalls, forests, plants and animals, that provide the deepest source of inspiration for Hawaiian music.

There are different theories about the beginnings of slack key guitar in the Islands. Music is one of the most mobile of cultural forms, and the six-string guitar was probably originally introduced to the Hawaiians by European sailors around the beginning of the 19th century.

Guitars were also brought to Hawaii by Mexican and Spanish vaqueros (cowboys), hired by King Kamehameha III around 1832 to teach the Hawaiians how to handle an overpopulation of cattle. In the evenings around the campfire, the vaqueros probably played their guitars, often two together, with one playing lead melody and the other bass and chords. This new instrument would have intrigued the Hawaiian cowboys, or paniolo, as they came to be called, who had their own strong, deep-rooted music traditions.

At first, there probably weren't a lot of guitars or people who knew how to play, so the Hawaiians developed a way to get a full sound on one guitar by picking the bass and rhythm chords on the lower three or four strings with the thumb, while playing the melody or improvised melodic fills on the upper two or three strings.

The slack key tradition was given an important boost during the reign of King David Kalakaua, who was responsible for the Hawaiian cultural resurgence of the 1880's and 1890's. He supported the preservation of ancient music, while encouraging the addition of imported instruments like the ukulele and guitar.

A wide variety of tunings in several different keys were created to back up the singers effectively. The Hawaiians often retuned the guitar from the standard Spanish tuning resulting in sweet sounding tunings with open strings.

The most influential slack key guitarist in history was Gabby Pahinui [1921-1980]. The modern slack key era began in 1947 when Gabby, "the father of modern slack key guitar" made his first recording of Hi'ilawe on an Aloha Records 78 rpm. Gabby was the prime influence for keeping slack key guitar from dying out in the Islands, and his prolific guitar techniques led to the guitar becoming more recognized as a solo instrument. Many have also been inspired by Gabby's beautiful, expressive vocals and his virtuoso falsetto voice.

Common Slack Key Tunings:

	Low to High			Low to High
Open D	D A D F# A D	C6		C G C G A E
D Wahine	D A D F# A C#	Old Mauna Loa		C G C G A D
G Major or Taro Patch	D G D G B D	Open C		C G C E G C
G Wahine	D G D F# B D	F Wahine		C F C G C E
C Major or Atta's	C G E G C E	Open F		C F C F A C
Mauna Loa	C G E G A E	Double Slack F		C F C E A C
C Wahine or Leonard's	C G D G B D			

Kaola Beamer contributed the next song, *No Ka Po*, it is deceptively simple yet fairly hard to play perfectly (I can attest to that). It's a beautiful composition and shows the common characteristics of the Slack Key guitar style.

NO KA PO
FOR THE NIGHT

F Wahine tuning

Kaola Beamer

Music gives a soul to the universe, wings to the mind, flight to the imagination, and life to everything.

Ritard
(second time)

(For time sake, I didn't use the repeats on the recording)

THE MARIMBA EFFECT (PALM HARMONICS):

A palm harmonic is created with the "Karate" side of your picking hand. If you rest that part of your hand on the 12th fret, you'll notice that the string doesn't vibrate where you're touching it, you can leave your hand on the strings and still hear a pitch, move your hand a half inch one way or the other and you'll hear the strings go dead. You have to twist your wrist so the skin on the side of your hand lines up with the frets. Leaving your hand on the strings mutes them a little and that helps to give it the wooden, Marimba effect (A Marimba is a Xylophone with wooden rather than metal bars and played with mallets). Then, of course, you have to play Latin type melodies. A Marimba player often plays with 2 mallets, so we need to use thirds to get that effect. Since palm harmonics don't come out as loud as regular notes, you'll have to turn up. (Turn up! When's the last time somebody said that to you?)

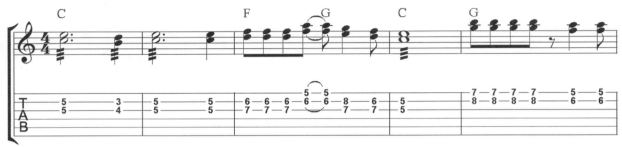

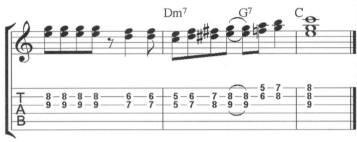

Most tapping licks tend to be played as triplets. The first note is hammered to the second and the third note is tapped. After a while, no matter how fast you can play them, they all start to sound the same. In an effort to change this, here is a 4 note pattern. What makes this one a little different is the use of 2 fingers on both hands. The sequence is tap, pull-off, tap, pull-off, one finger at a time. The second finger of the picking hand taps a note and pulls it off to the second finger of the other hand, then repeat with the first finger of each hand. Lift each finger after using it. As always, *experiment!* (P.H. = picking hand, F.H. = fretting hand)

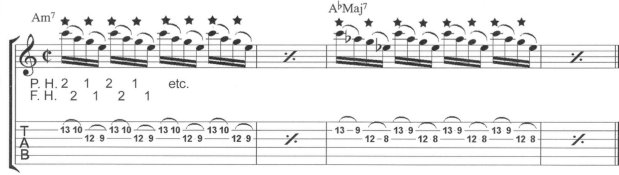

Rockabilly rhythm guitar almost always uses either or both of these melodies. Sometimes it's all the rhythm player would play. No chords, just these melodies.

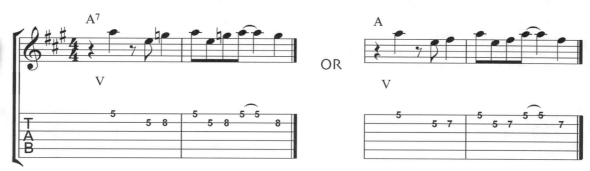

OR

Often, the guitarist would take a more fingerpicking approach to the rhythm pattern. A thumb pick will definitely help give this example more punch. Keeping a rock solid thumb pattern is the secret to making this sound good. Work on it slowly and be very precise.

The whole note A under the staff is a notational short cut that means let everything in the measure ring out.

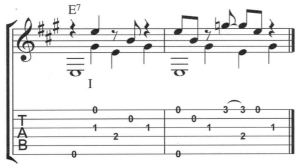

SPREAD TRIAD ARPEGGIOS:

Jon Finn donated this example that shows you a new way of playing triad arpeggios. Using the arpeggio of a spread voiced major triad (see ex. 76 for more) he goes between an A and a G major triad and plays them over an A⁷ chord. It's a cool open sound used by other players like Eric Johnson and it will add a new dimension to your arpeggio playing. Watch Jon play this and other examples in the video folder. Open "Jon Finn." Use alternate picking throughout.

continue back up the neck playing the arpeggios in the reverse order.

Again, it's all about the shapes. In this Jazz lick, you start by going up an Fmaj⁷ arpeggio which is nice and smooth, then you break it up with 2 note groups that leap around until they resolve chromatically to the 3rd of the Gm⁷ chord.

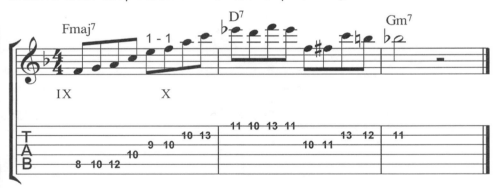

An interesting augmented lick can be created by just running the augmented triad arpeggios up and down a whole step away from each other. Since the G⁷♯5 chord can take a whole tone scale, you can play almost anything and move it around by whole steps. Use "arpeggio picking" for this example. That means, all up strokes for the first 4 notes, slide down and then all down strokes for the next 3 notes. Don't let any notes ring into each other.

A Blues comping rhythm using triads. You've probably heard this before from the piano player, well, here it is for us. There are 3 main inversions of a minor triad (in this case, F#m and Em, which end up sounding like A^6 and A^9) that we can use whenever we want in a blues progression. In measures 3 and 4 you'll find all 3 inversions available on the A^7 chord. Once you know them, just transpose them to the other chords in the progression. I've added a pedal point root to make it sound bigger, but the triads will work fine without the bass note when you're in keys that don't have open string roots available. The low notes with the slash through the stem are a notational shortcut for repeated eighth notes.

This open string lick is a little different. Ex. 21 and 120 showed a similar fingering for a Country style lick in D, but when you move it down a fret, it turns into a harmonic minor lick. How convenient! You can use this in Country (although there's not a lot of situations where a harmonic minor scale is called for) or in Jazz to add some spice to an otherwise boring scale lick.

DADGAD - ALTERNATE TUNING:

This is an excerpt from Phil Keaggy's beautiful composition entitled *County Down* from his award winning album *Beyond Nature* available at www.philkeaggy.com. This small example is just the tip of the iceberg as far as this tune and the DADGAD tuning goes. With a little experimenting, you'll be able to find a lot of great sounding new chord voicings you've never played before. Some other tunings Phil uses are: (from low to high) D A D F♯ B D (D6), E G♯ E G♯ C♯ E (E6), D A D G B E (drop D), E B C♯ G B E (Em6) and many more. Open "Phil Keaggy" in the video folder to hear him play this example as well as other wonderful alternate tuning compositions.

If the Fmaj7 is a IV chord then this Lydian Jazz lick fits perfectly. If it's a I chord, you're forcing ♯11 into a scale where it doesn't belong. But, if it's the last chord of the song, it's OK to do it. Actually you can play it whenever you want. The previous statement is just me following the rules for chord scales. Out there in the real world, this lick sounds cool on all major7 chords at all times.

COUNTRY MUSIC - A BRIEF HISTORY:

Country music is a blend of popular musical forms originally found in the Southern United States. It has roots in traditional Folk, Celtic, Blues, Gospel, and old-time music and it evolved in the 1920's. The term Country Music actually is an umbrella for several different styles of music including *The Nashville Sound, Bluegrass, Western,* which includes traditional Western cowboy campfire ballads and Hollywood cowboy music made famous by Roy Rogers, The Sons of the Pioneers, and Gene Autry, *Western Swing,* dance music popularized by Bob Wills, *The Bakersfield Sound,* which used the new Fender Telecaster guitars and a big drum beat, *Outlaw Country,* made famous in the 1970's by Waylon Jennings, Willie Nelson, Kris Kristofferson, Merle Haggard, Hank Williams and others, *Cajun* style music from the Louisiana Bayou, *Zydeco, Evangelical Christian Gospel, Oldtime* (generally pre-1930 folk music), *Honky Tonk, Appalachian, Rockabilly,* and *Jug Band.*
Jimmie Rodgers and the Carter Family are widely considered to be the founders of Country music, and their songs were first captured at a historic recording session in Bristol, Tennessee on August 1, 1927.

During the 1960's, Country music became a multimillion-dollar industry centered in Nashville, Tennessee. Under the direction of producers such as Chet Atkins and Owen Bradley, the Nashville Sound brought country music to a diverse audience. This sound was notable for borrowing from 1950's pop songs using a smooth vocal singing style backed by a string section and vocal chorus. Instrumental soloing was less important in favor of trademark licks. Leading artists in this style included Patsy Cline, Jim Reeves, and later Tammy Wynette and Charlie Rich. Although Country music has a lot of styles, many think they were all homogenized by the producers that created the Nashville Sound. Others point to the commercial need to re-invent Country in the face of the dominance of 50's Rock 'n' Roll and the subsequent British Invasion. Even today, people still think of Country music as having all the stereotypes of hillbillies, nasal sounding vocalists and tear jerking ballads.

The old joke is: "What do you get when you play a Country song backwards? You get your truck back, your dog back, your wife back, your house back..."

The two types of country music that have continued to develop since the 1990's are the Jimmie Rodgers influence, which can be seen in the "working man" image of singers like Brooks & Dunn and Garth Brooks and The Carter Family style which has been continued by singers like Iris Dement and Nanci Griffith who have written more traditional "folk" themes, but with a modern point of view.

In the mid 1990's Country music was taken over by the line dancing craze which continues today. In the late 1990's a new form of Country music called by some Alternative Country began to be performed by younger musicians. It shunned the Nashville dominated sound of mainstream Country and borrowed more from Rock groups than the watered-down pop of Nashville.

After the FM radio stations became stylistic singularities like Country, Oldies, Classic Rock, Smooth Jazz, Easy Listening etc etc. it's become hard to find any traditional country music to listen to. The bulk of radio airplay today is whatever Nashville thinks is new and will sell records. If Willie Nelson and Johnny Cash tried to get a record deal today, do you think they'd be signed?

A very incomplete list of the most important Country guitarists include: Chet Atkins, Merle Travis, Joe Maphis, Albert Lee, Maybelle Carter, Doc Watson, Ricky Scaggs, Danny Gatton, Ray Flacke, Hank Garland, Jimmy Bryant, Jerry Reed, Junior Brown, James Burton, Vince Gill, Brad Paisley, Jerry Donahue, Brent Mason, Steve Wariner and many, many more. Do a search for these players to learn more about their music.

Silence is the fabric upon which the notes are woven.

310

THE TUNING FORK:

In this age of electronic tuners, many forget about the humble little tuning fork.

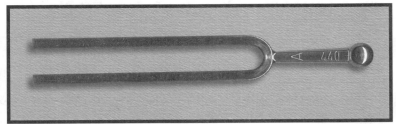

First of all, no batteries required, it works at all times under all circumstances. "But I can't always hear it," you say. Here's how to deal with that.

1. Hit it on your knee while holding the small end then bring the vibrating fork part directly over one of your pickups (make sure that pickup is turned on). You'll hear it loud and clear through your amp.

2. For acoustic guitar, hit the fork part on your knee and place the small end on the top of your guitar's body. The body will resonate with the fork's pitch.

3. Still can't hear it? Hit it on your knee and put the small end on your teeth! Your entire head will vibrate with the fork's pitch!

They come in many pitches, but for guitar, get either an A or an E fork.

Not a tuning fork thing, but cool nonetheless, if you want to hear your electric guitar better but can't get to an amp, place the headstock of your guitar against a wall or a hollow door and you'll amplify the guitar enough for it to be heard surprisingly well.

Only become a musician if there is absolutely no other way you can make a living.

311

This Jazz example shows a nice use of the concept of using guide tones (see ex. 147) to connect the chords. You can't go wrong starting each measure on either the 3rd or 7th of the chord.

Let's take this melody apart. It starts on the major 7th of the F chord, works its way down to the 3rd on the D^7 chord, arpeggios up to the $\flat 9$ and $\sharp 9$ then turns around and comes down to the 3rd on the G^7 chord using the guide tone resolution of 7 to 3, it then arpeggios up to the 13th on the C^7 and resolves to the root of the F chord.

Here is a more complicated version of the Country rhythm example found in ex.290. Measure 8 has a touch of that Bluegrass sound because of the B♭ ringing against the B natural. Make sure all the hammer-ons and pull-offs are played with a little extra strength to make them loud enough. All chords are open chords in the first position. Remember, a number inside a circle tells you the string a note is on (measure 8).

Pop Rock Ballad rhythm guitar often uses a sixteenth note light funky feel. I may have overwritten this example, but I wanted to include as many different rhythms as possible. Let the chords ring out most of the time, until you have to let them go in order to play the X's. The accents give it a little life. This is the rhythm part for ex. 221.

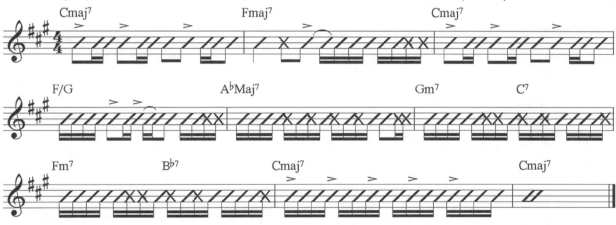

This Blues lick pushes the solo forward. It could be the first bar or the last. As the opening lick, you could play it like a theme to carry you through the entire 12 bars. As the last measure, the lick would signify to the band and the audience that you're not ready to stop yet and you want to play another 12 bars. It's standard procedure, and usually not notated, to bend the B♭'s up a quarter step each time they appear.

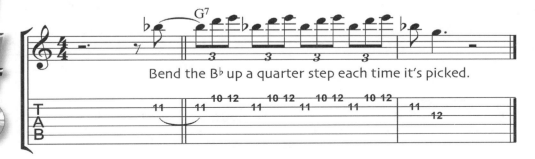

Bend the B♭ up a quarter step each time it's picked.

SURF MUSIC:

In the early 60's the youth movement was looking for something new. Rock 'n' Roll was catching on and the surfing craze in California was getting bigger every day. That "something new" turned out to be guitar based instrumentals. There hadn't been many Rock instrumentals up to that point but when groups like The Surfaris *Wipeout* 1962, The Chantays *Pipeline* 1963, Dick Dale, The Ventures and The Shadows (in England) reached #1 on the charts, their place in Surf music history was assured. Lead, rhythm, bass and drums was the line up for all these bands and Surf music was the first genre to universally accept electric bass. The development of the drum kit style evolved from Surf music as much as it did from Rock. Fender guitars were the main guitars of the style. The most popular was the Fender Jaguar and its distinct sound helped give Surf music its unique sonic flavor. Crank up the spring reverb, shout "Cowabunga" and jump in...surf's up!

Here is a good Blues or Fusion lick. The first 2 measures use a C major pentatonic scale instead of the C blues scale you'd expect. Then you go up 4 different major triad arpeggios (C, B♭, E♭ and G♭) finally bending into the high E. A little crunch in you sound helps this one sing.

This minor pentatonic lick works well in Rock or Blues. It's fairly easy to play fast because of all the hammers and pull-offs. If you try picking every single note, you'll see what I mean. Hammers and pull-offs are our friends!

An altered chord means the chord must contain a flat or sharp 5 plus a flat or sharp 9. Use either flat or sharp, but you can't use natural 5 or 9 in the voicing. The altered dominant chord scale contains these changes to a major scale: 1, ♭9, ♯9, 3, ♭5, ♯5 and ♭7. A very complicated scale to say the least. Luckily, it's exactly the same as the seventh mode of the melodic minor scale. In this case, B♭ melodic minor is played from its 7th degree over the A⁷ altered chord. If you want to sound "hip", play the altered scale over any dominant seventh chord even when it's not written as altered.

WESTERN SWING - A BRIEF HISTORY:

Western Swing is aimed at dancers. Much of it is played with an up-tempo beat. It consists of a combination of Country, Polka, Gypsy Jazz, Mexican, and Folk music, blended with a jazzy swing, a touch of New Orleans Jazz and Blues, and today is played by a band made up of a typical rhythm section (piano, guitar, bass and drums), twin fiddles (2 fiddles playing in harmony) and a steel guitar, the steel is usually a double or triple neck non-pedal guitar.

This genre originated in the dance halls of small towns throughout the Lower Great Plains in the 1920's and 1930's. Bob Wills (The King of Western Swing) and his Texas Playboys essentially created this stylistic blend in the early 1930's. He played dance-halls all over the southwest and took advantage of the new medium of radio broadcasting which helped the style gain a much wider following.

Western Swing reached its "golden age" during the years preceding WWII, blossomed on the West Coast during the War, and was extremely popular throughout the West. Its decline in the years following the War seemed to mirror the drop in popularity of the more mainstream big-band sound. The capital of Western Swing has always been, Austin, Texas.

Musically, the country players tried to emulate the sound of the big bands like those of Benny Goodman, Count Basie and Duke Ellington. The early versions of Bob Wills' band actually had as many as 18 members and was, in essence, a full size big band. As the sound evolved, the size of the band was reduced to between 8 and 10 players. The improvised solo lines, played by the fiddles, guitar and steel, were all stock Jazz/Bebop phrases but the rhythm section played much simpler than their big band counterparts. Bass players often just used roots and fifths and when they walked, they tended to play roots on each new chord. Jazz bassists would walk through those chords and have other scale degrees in the bass rather than the root. Drums were even more basic and played what might be described as a swinging polka beat.

Some classic Western Swing songs include, *San Antonio Rose, Steel Guitar Rag, Roly Poly, Take Me Back to Tulsa, Home in San Antone* and *Stay a Little Longer*.

Carrying on the Western Swing tradition today are bands like *Asleep at the Wheel* and *Commander Cody and His Lost Planet Airmen*.

For those times when you have 2 measures to fill before your solo starts and you can't think of anything to play, this one works great. It's strange enough to get people's attention and hip enough to make you sound cool. The lick is based on major triad arpeggios a tritone away from each other. It works because the substitute dominant chord for any chord is a tritone (an augmented 4th or diminished 5th) away from the original chord. This one will fit into almost any style but Folk.

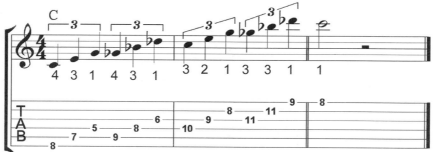

Here's one of those neo-classical Metal licks that use the concept of a pedal point where one note moves downward against a higher pitch that doesn't move. Play as fast as possible. Thanks to Joe Stump for this one.

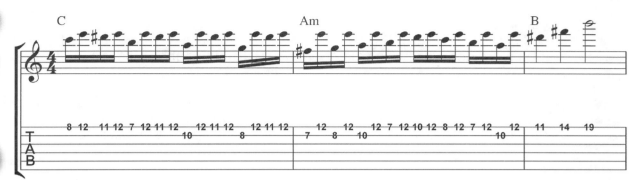

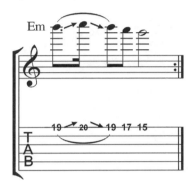

Except for a few chromatic approaches, this Jazz example is all arpeggios and scales. The opening arpeggio doesn't just go up 1, ♭3, 5, ♭7, it goes up ♭3, 5, ♭7, 9, and 11 using all the "good" notes. The last measure uses 9, 7 and 5. The point is, when you play an arpeggio, go for the higher numbered tensions, they will always sound better than the lower ones.

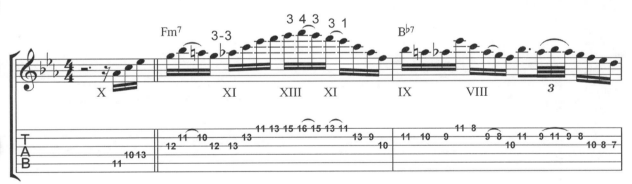

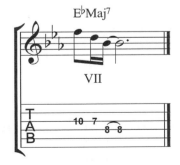

As I've mentioned before, Harmonics occur 12, 7 and 5 frets above any note. There are others, but these are the most usable. This example uses the 7-frets-above harmonic to get notes that aren't obviously available in the chord being played.

As a student at Berklee, I was writing a chord solo on the tune *Misty* and wanted a big ending. I used this fairly common descending chord progression from the IV down to the I chord. But, after I played the last E$\flat$6 chord, I really wanted to hear the opening melody again as harmonics. The problem was that the opening notes of *Misty*, (B$\flat$, G and D) were not present in that chord. After thinking about it for a while, I found that playing artificial harmonics 7 frets above the chord gave me the notes I needed. The E$\flat$ (2nd string) gave me a B$\flat$, the C (3rd string) gave the note G and the low G (4th string) produced the note D. There it was, all the notes I needed to make a nice ending and I never would have thought of it if I didn't know about playing harmonics 7 frets away from the fingered pitches (I got an "A" on my chord solo).

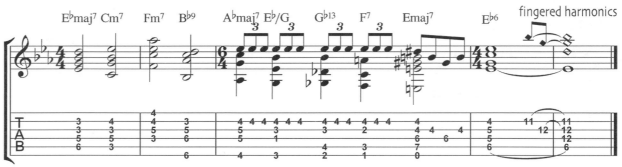

Whenever you see a dom7#5 or dom7aug chord, one of the scales you can use is the whole tone scale. That's the scale used in this Jazz example and the first 4 notes build a repetitive pattern. You play the first 4 notes going from high to low, then move back 2 frets and play the same thing from low to high. Keep this up until the chromatic approaches to the 3rd of the B$\flat$maj7 chord.

If you don't like the sound of the symmetric whole tone scale, you can treat the chord as if it were a dom7$\flat$13 and play a melodic minor scale up a fourth, in this case it would be a B$\flat$ melodic minor scale or an F mixolydian $\flat$6 mode. Try substituting that scale and see how it sounds.

SMOKING IS BAD FOR YOU: I'm riding with the band in an RV from somewhere in Pennsylvania back to Boston. Being a smoker (at the time) whenever they would stop for gas, I would jump out and have a smoke. It's the middle of the night, everybody in the RV is sleeping, the 2 guys in the front pull in for gas so I get out for a smoke. Little did I know, they were just changing places as drivers and didn't notice that I went out the side door. They got back in and took off! I'm running and whistling but they didn't see or hear me. I was stranded! Cold and alone (sigh). I called the State Troopers and told them to pull over the RV and tell them to come back and get me, but the RV had already exited from the highway to drop off the bass player. When they stopped to let him out, they noticed I wasn't in the RV and finally, about 2 hours later, came back to get me! Like I said, smoking is bad for you!

THE HARP SOUND EFFECT:

No one knows who came up with this effect first, but Chet Atkins was certainly one of the first to use it on a recording. Lenny Breau continued to develop the technique and took it to an even higher level of complexity. The basic concept is to have 6 notes ring together and still be more or less within the same octave. In order to do this, you must play half of them as fingered harmonics (see ex.159 for fingered harmonics). This brings them up an octave and places them inside the non-harmonic notes creating the illusion that all the notes are ringing out together side by side. Any six note chord without any doubled notes will work with this technique. It helps if you have a nail on your ring finger to match the sound of the pick attack. Here are 2 of my favorite voicings.

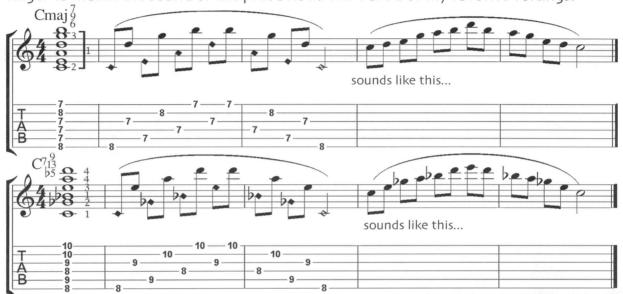

sounds like this...

sounds like this...

THE SITAR:

This instrument is probably the best known South Asian instrument in the West. It is a Hindustani classical stringed instrument which utilizes sympathetic strings along with regular strings and a gourd resonating chamber to produce a very distinctive sound. The sitar has been prevalent in Hindustani classical music

Tony Karasek co-designer - Photo by Brian Dering

since the Middle Ages. It became popular in the West when The Beatles used it in many songs, including *Norwegian Wood, Across the Universe, Tomorrow Never Knows,* and *Within You Without You.* Beatles lead guitarist George Harrison was inspired by, and later taught by, sitar player extraodinaire, Ravi Shankar.

The 7 main strings   The 13 sympathetic strings

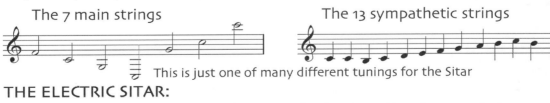

This is just one of many different tunings for the Sitar

THE ELECTRIC SITAR:

The guitar is played and tuned like a standard guitar. The characteristic buzzing effect is achieved as the strings vibrate over a carved rosewood "table" acting as the bridge, approximately 1½" long. The 13 sympathetic drone strings (all plain .010 gauge) can be tuned to chords or scales of one's choice, starting in the range one octave above the open top E string. They have their own pickup, volume and tone controls.

PLAYING IN OCTAVES:

Wes Montgomery is the king of playing in octaves. His laid back Jazz/Blues style has become the benchmark for all guitarists who want to learn how to play in this style. Like most players that are famous for one technique or another, Wes didn't invent to concept, he just became well known for it.

The technique is fairly simple in theory but not so easy to play. The sound comes from using the side of your thumb and strumming the octaves. Unlike using pick and fingers with octaves to avoid the sound of the dead string between the notes, with this style you actually want to hear that dead string in the strum. In fact, Wes strummed all 6 stirngs instead of just the 3 you might expect.

When playing in octaves, it's next to impossible to play any fast runs, but that's not a negative thing, it forces you to think more about the melodies you create and less about all the cool hot licks you might know.

I find it easier to watch the lower note as I play rather than the high note. It really doesn't matter which you choose as long as you can see where you're going.

In the example, the next to last measure has the octave with a fourth in it. This sound has been greatly expanded upon by George Benson and I suggest you listen to him to hear how he uses it in his soloing. It's a very exciting sound when played properly. Some grace notes are shown but feel free to add more. Sliding into an octave from a half step below is a common technique in this style.

Be sure to watch Richie Hart's performance in the video folder. Open "Richie Hart." He does a great job of playing and explaining the styles of Wes Montgomery and George Benson.

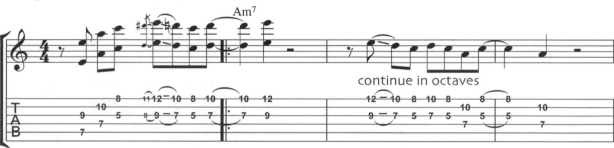

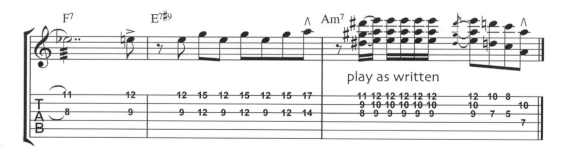

After silence, that which comes nearest to expressing the inexpressible is music.

BLUEGRASS MUSIC - A BRIEF HISTORY:

Bluegrass music is considered a form of American roots music with its own roots in English, Irish and Scottish traditional music. The name of the genre is derived from the Blue Grass Boys, the name of Bill Monroe's band. Like Jazz, Bluegrass is played with each melody instrument switching off, playing improvised solos in turn while the others revert to backing the soloist. This is in contrast to old-time music, in which all instruments play the melody together or one instrument carried the lead throughout while the others provide accompaniment.

Unlike mainstream Country music, Bluegrass relies mostly on acoustic stringed instruments. The fiddle, banjo, acoustic guitar, mandolin, and upright bass are sometimes joined by the resonator guitar or Dobro and drums were not introduced until recently. This instrumentation originated in rural black dance bands and was being abandoned by those groups in favor of Blues and Jazz when it was picked up by white musicians. Instrumental solos are improvised, and can frequently be technically demanding.

As with any musical genre, no one person can claim to have "invented" it. Rather, Bluegrass is a mixture of old-time music, Blues, Ragtime and Jazz. Nevertheless, the beginning of Bluegrass music can be traced to one band. Today, Bill Monroe is referred to as the "founding father" of Bluegrass music. The 1945 addition to the band of banjo player Earl Scruggs, who played with a three-finger roll originally developed by Snuffy Jenkins but now almost universally known as "Scruggs style," is said to be the defining moment in the development of Bluegrass music. Monroe's 1945-48 band, which featured banjo player Earl Scruggs, singer/guitarist Lester Flatt, fiddler Chubby Wise and bassist Howard Watts, created the definitive sound and instrumental configuration that remains intact to this day.

Besides instrumentation, one of the other distinguishing characteristics of Bluegrass is the vocal harmonies featuring two, three or four parts, an emphasis on traditional songs, often with sentimental or religious themes. This vocal style has been characterized as the "high lonesome sound." This sound has a nasal quality to the voice, and is sung over the main melody. There is usually no vibrato in the singers voice. They would often choose a harmony part a fourth or fifth away from the melody rather than going to the nearest third as one might do in a traditional Country or Pop song.

Prominent and influential players and bands include Bill Monroe and his Blue Grass Boys, the Stanley Brothers, Lester Flatt & Earl Scruggs with the Foggy Mountain Boys, The Dillards, Norman Blake, Tony Rice, Dan Crary, Del McCoury, Ricky Scaggs, Alison Krauss, Bela Fleck and the Flecktones, Alison Brown and Mark O'connor. This is by no means a complete list of Bluegrass players. You are encouraged to do a search for others and listen to as many as possible to learn more about this style.

TRICKS OF THE TRADE: My brother Albert, in Beverly Hills, California, asked me to supply him with a 5 minute music track with a lonesome harmonica playing against a background of waves rolling up onto the beach plus the sound of a fog horn and a buoy in the distance. The sound effects were easy enough with my library of pre-recorded sounds but getting a convincing harmonica sound, without using an actual harmonica player, was a bit harder. My Yamaha synth had a good harmonica sound but it was missing that "wa wa" you get from using your hands. *I had an idea!* I recorded the harmonica part, dubbed it down to a cassette (you remember those...plastic things with recording tape inside of them) and played it back through the cassette deck's headphones. Then I took the padding off the headphone's earpiece so that all that was left was the little speaker. I cupped the speaker in my hands and as the track played, I held my hands up to a studio mic and did the open and close hand movemnets which gave it a *very* realistic sound. Needless to say, my brother was impressed!

PEDAL STEEL GUITAR:

Basically, the pedal steel comes in two varieties, a single neck and a double neck. A single neck steel always uses the E^9th tuning (used mainly for Country licks) and the second neck adds the C^6 tuning (used mostly in Jazz and Western Swing). There are 10 strings per neck and a variable amount of pedals and knee levers to change the pitch of the strings. Although many people were trying to figure out a good way to stretch and loosen the strings on a steel guitar, the first major leap was when Paul A. Bigsby started to build pedal steels for Speedy West, Merle Travis, Ernie Ball and other great players. His guitars set the standard for tone and quality from 1946 to 1958. In 1945, an incredible little pedal steel guitar was designed and mass produced by the Harlin Brothers of Indianapolis, Indiana. It was called the Multi-Kord and was truly a work of art for its day. This was the first 3 piece finger mechanism all pull steel guitar ever built. It was built very inexpensively. In 1949, Bigsby added pedals to Speedy West's triple 8 string steel guitar that worked very well. However, pedal steel guitar was pretty much still a novelty until Webb Pierce recorded *Slowly*. This was a number one tune in the early to mid 50's. *Slowly* was recorded with Bud Isaacs playing his double neck 8 string, 2 pedal Bigsby guitar. In 1958, several players who could not get a guitar like the one Isaacs used because of the 3 year waiting list, bought a guitar called the Sho-Bud built by Shot Jackson and Sons and promoted by Buddy Emmons and later, in the mid-sixties, by Buddy Charlton. The significant guitars down through history are Rickenbacher, Electrodaire, Multi-Kord, Bigsby, Fender 1000 (and 400), Sho-Bud, Emmons and the new wave of GFI-Magnum guitars. There are many other fine brands of steels like Mullen, Derby, Williams, JCH, Performance, Rittenberry, MSA, Fessenden and Carter.

Players to listen to include Bobby Black, Tom Brumley, Noel Boggs, Buddy Cage, Chuck Campbell, Curly Chalker, BJ Cole, Pete Drake, Buddy Emmons, Neil Flanz, Paul Franklin, Jerry Garcia, Lloyd Green, John Hughey, Bud Isaacs, Doug Jernigan, Sarah Jory, Leon McAuliffe, Weldon Myrick, Jeff Newman, Robert Randolph, Alvino Rey, Bobbe Seymour, Herby Wallace and Speedy West to name just a few. In the example below, the quarter notes are the open strings and the notes in parenthesis are the pitches you can go to with the pedals and knee levers. Yes, the top 2 strings are lower than the 3rd string. They're there to make scale passages easier to play.

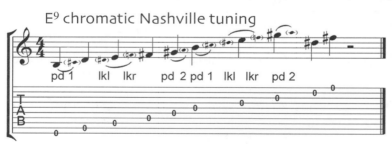

E^9 chromatic Nashville tuning

lkl means left knee lever moving to the left
lkr means left knee lever moving to the right.

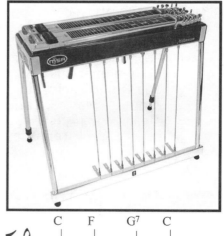

In this example, you can see how easy it is to do a simple I-IV-V-I progression by just using the appropriate pedals and knee levers. The beauty of the way the pedals and knee levers work is that you can play any of the basic string groups and they will all be affected by the pedals and knee levers in the same way. Since a plastic thumb pick and 2 metal finger picks are used, 3 note voicings are common. The basic string groups are, 10-8-6, 8-6-5, 6-5-4, 5-4-3.

When writing for pedal steel, the safest thing to do is to just write chord changes. Reading single notes is difficult, only include them when absolutely necessary. A good player will add the right licks without you having to write any of them out.

PEDAL STEEL continued

I'd say about 80 percent of the steel guitar licks you hear in a Country tune are played by just using the first 2 pedals. In this classic lick, you start with pedal 2 down then rock the first pedal on, release it and repeat.

This typical ending lick shows that the last 2 chords are played by simply going from no pedals to pedals 1 and 2. Pretty easy. The hard part of pedal steel is the right hand. You have to learn how to block almost every note you play because the bar just lays there covering the strings. If you don't want all the notes to ring together (and you don't) then you have to block them. The second example shows some of the other types of chords available with the E9th tuning.

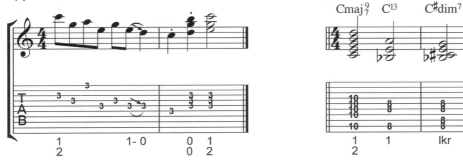

The C6th tuning is a much lower pitched tuning and is really built for Jazz and Western Swing. 5 pedals and 2 to 4 knee levers have become standard on the C6 neck but players have lots of other additions that make their set-up unique. Here's Buddy Emmons' layout on his C6 neck. The second example shows some of the Jazz chords that are easy to find with this tuning.

(Thanks to Bobbe Seymour for the history of the Pedal Steel)

THE NASHVILLE NUMBER SYSTEM:

In the world of mainstream Jazz and Pop music, we write charts with chord progressions like Cmaj^7, Dm^7, Bm^{7b5}, etc. We talk and write about them using Roman numerals like I, IIm^7 and VIIm^{7b5}. This is normal for much of written music, but in Nashville, they do it a bit differently. First of all, they threw out the Roman numerals and replaced them with plain old Arabic numbers. Someone might describe a song by saying, "The verse is a fifteen eleven with a forty four fifty five and the chorus is a forty four sixteen with a twenty three forty five." What that means to a song in the key of C is to play (one measure each) C, G^7, C, C, F, F, G^7, G^7, the chorus would be F, F, C, A, D, E, F, G^7.

In our system, we have the pattern of maj, min, min, maj, dom, min, min^{7b5} made by the diatonic chords. The NNS (Nashville Number System) presumes every chord is a major chord unless you're told otherwise. If you wanted a C, Am, Dm, G, you'd have to write 1, 6-, 2-, 5. The "m" (lower case m) is occasionally used for minor but since it could be misread as major, they usually use the "-" dash to mean minor.

The one thing the NNS does a little weird is the way they notate a chord over a bass note. We're used to seeing C, G/B, Am, Am/G, they would write it as 1, 5/7, 6-, 6-/5. They call the bass note by it's scale degree number *not* by it's relationship to the chord. It's not a G chord with it's 3rd in the bass (B) it's a G chord over the 7th degree of the C scale. That takes a little getting used to.

One number equals one measure of that chord. Numbers that are either underlined, put in parenthesis or surrounded in a box are 2 beats each. If there are 4 numbers in the box, they're a quarter beat each. If you want a half beat for one chord and quarter beats for the other two, you'd put 2 dots over the first chord and one dot over each of the other two chords.

They use repeat signs, D.S. al coda and other normal "road map" indications (see the bottom of ex. 183 for more on "road maps"). It's always best to write out the entire tune rather than have a verse and chorus followed by a long list of directions telling you to play the verse twice then the chorus once then the verse once etc. etc.

If you want to know more about the NNS, the best book available is called, "The Nashville Number System" by Chas Williams. It's available from his web site, www.nashvillenumbersystem.com. Here's an example of the tune *Crazy* using the NNS.

Here are a few more examples of the harp harmonic licks that Lenny Breau and others have made famous. This technique works on almost any chord that has all 6 strings in it. You'll have to learn a few new voicings since most of our chord forms only cover 4 or 5 strings. The second and third example include an extra note via the hammer-on and this adds another half step to the harmony which sounds great.

These are all wonderful by themselves but if you string them together in the order they're shown, you'll have a really nice chord progression. As an alternative to pick and fingers, using a thumb pick will give a nice clear attack. You still need to have a little bit of fingernail on your other fingers to get an equal attack to that of the thumbpick.

Another Snappin' and Slappin' example (see ex. 127 and 295 for more). If you have an out of phase position with your pickups, like position 2 and 5 on a strat, it will help this technique sound brighter and funkier.

Someone once asked me if I had seen what was written above the urinal on the wall in the fifth floor bathroom of the 1140 Boylston Street building at Berklee. I hadn't, so I went to see for myself, worried about what it might say. What was written was not only clever but almost inspirational.

"As I go through life, let my conscience be Mike Ihde"

(It could have been a lot worse!)

SINGING AND PLAYING AT THE SAME TIME:

If you think you'll get a lot of work just because you can play a lot of licks and play them fast, think again. There are way too many guitarists out there that can play rings around you. So what can you do to make yourself more saleable? First and foremost, be a singing guitar player. Secondly, learn to play other instruments like the pedal steel, lap steel, bass guitar, banjo, mandolin, etc. (If it has strings on it, you should be able to play it!)

Of all the work I do around New England, maybe 40 percent is because I'm a good guitar player, 10 percent because I play other instruments and the remaining 50 percent is because I can sing. I don't sing great, I'll never be discovered and given a record deal because of my voice, but I can sing in tune and I've learned how to "sell" a song to the audience. I've also learned how to accompany myself, so singing and playing at the same time is not a problem.

The secret to doing two things at once is simple. You must know the rhythm part perfectly without having to think about what you're doing. Most people have trouble because they're still thinking about what the next chord is. Practice the tune until you can play it in your sleep. Then, and only then, can you sing along with the rhythm part without thinking about what your hands are doing.

Start with a simple tune like *Proud Mary* with an uncomplicated rhythm pattern like this:

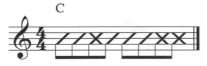

After you feel comfortable with that rhythm, make it a little more complex like this:

Then, make it a lot harder with a funky rhythm like this one from the tune *Get Ready*.

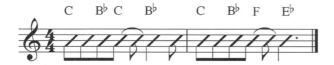

A lot of today's singer/songwriters strum simple rhythms to back themselves up. Go back to the classics like The Beatles *Blackbird*, The Temptations *My Girl*, or even The Monkees *Last Train to Clarksville* (that's a hard one). Don't be stuck in a style. Just because you think you sound your best singing Black Sabbeth tunes, learn some Country, Funk, Blues or Jazz standards as well. The more songs you can sing (no lyric pages allowed on the gig!) and the better you can accompany yourself, the more work you'll get, guaranteed.

INDEX

COUNTRY-BLUEGRASS-FOLK-WESTERN SWING-ROCKABILLY:

ROCK-BLUES-FUNK-R&B-POP-METAL:

JAZZ-FUSION:

TECHNIQUES:

TRICKS AND OTHER STUFF: